Everyday Cake

45 Simple Recipes for LAYER, BUNDT, LOAF, and SHEET CAKES

POLINA CHESNAKOVA

Photography by Charity Burggraaf

 SASQUATCH BOOKS
SEATTLE

CONTENTS

INTRODUCTION

Whether right after a meal, while winding down in the evening, or when we gather with friends and loved ones, my family always pours tea—and what is that hot, steaming cup without something sweet to accompany it? This was how I was introduced at an early age to the pleasure of a simple dessert, often cake. Drawn in not so much by the sugar, but by a deep satisfaction that stems from "that ideal match of the right dish and the right moment," as the restaurateur and cookbook author Yotam Ottolenghi said.

That idea is what *Everyday Cake* is all about—cakes in all shapes and forms for every mood and occasion. Maybe a long day at work necessitates a treat, an unexpected guest stops in, or you're looking to celebrate, but without too much fuss. In other words, day-to-day moments that warrant a spark of joy.

In these pages, you'll find cakes that are neither overly complicated nor too sweet but *are* reliably delicious. Some, like the Lemon-Lavender Yogurt Cake (page 143), are a one-bowl magic trick, while others call for layers (never more than two!) and frosting, like the Yellow Birthday Cake with Whipped Malt Chocolate Buttercream (page 91). There are a handful, such as the Salted Butterscotch Fudge Sheet Cake (page 127), that feed a crowd, but many more will be easily tackled by a party of two. And if your style, like mine, skews classic with a twist, then you'll especially love the Golden-Milk Tres Leches Cake (page 111) and the Sour Cream Coffee Cake with Five-Spice Streusel (page 26).

The chapters are organized by the forms the cakes are baked in—Bundt and tube; round; square and rectangular; and loaf pans—because I find each shape carries its own vibe and associations. (A Chocolate Sour Cream Cake on page 145 keeps it casual, while a Sugared Jelly Donut Bundt Cake on page 35 begs to be served at brunch.) My recipes are clear and detailed, meant to empower—not overwhelm—the reader. Throughout the book, tidbits of pastry know-how will address any questions you might have in the process and leave you smarter in the kitchen too.

My hope is that whether you're a novice or seasoned baker, or somewhere in between, this cookbook will entice you and bring delight no matter the reason. So next time your day calls for a sweet treat, let *Everyday Cake* be the answer.

LET'S GET STARTED

BAKING TIPS

Read First

Before you start making a recipe, read it all the way through—preferably twice. Make note of what needs to be done ahead of time, any potentially tricky or time-sensitive steps, the ingredients and equipment you'll need, which ingredients are divided and when to add them, etc. Having a good sense of a recipe's flow of preparation is key.

Gather Second

Mise en place is the French phrase for "everything in its place." Once you've read the recipe, gather your on-hand equipment and ingredients and make a list of what you'll need to buy. Before proceeding, make sure the ingredients are at the temperature called for; then measure and set them out accordingly. Preheat the oven as specified in the recipe, and don't forget to prep your pan! Unless you're baking a Bundt cake (see page 21), feel free to use either melted butter or shortening, nonstick baking spray, or oil for greasing.

Use a Kitchen Scale

A digital scale is the easiest way to improve your baking. One cup of measured flour can weigh anywhere from 120 to 140 grams depending on how one measures it. Compound that with varying weights for other ingredients, and you might end up with a drastically different cake than expected. Not only will you bake with confidence knowing that you're using the exact amounts called for in the recipe, but it will also streamline your ingredient prep (no more fumbling with measuring cups!).

Spoon and Sweep

In the recipes that follow, 1 cup of all-purpose flour weighs 130 grams. If you don't have a kitchen scale, use the spoon-and-sweep method. Fluff up the flour, spoon it into the measuring cup, then sweep the top with the flat edge of a knife—this helps prevent the flour from getting too densely packed and ensures consistent results. This is also how I measure my sugars, cocoa powder, and other dry ingredients.

Mix It Up

These recipes were tested with a stand mixer. If you don't have one, a powerful, multisetting hand mixer and a large bowl will do, but please note:

BE PATIENT: Everything, from creaming butter to whipping egg whites, will take longer—sometimes twice as long. Rely on visual and tactile cues in addition to time estimates.

BE MINDFUL: Small appliances require more physical effort on your part—be sure to move the beaters around to the edges of the bowl, as well as work them through the center for even, thorough mixing.

BE DISCERNING: Unfortunately, when it comes to whipping large amounts of egg whites (say, a dozen) or very gently stirring a dough, hand mixers can't do it all. Listen to your gut and either shelve the recipe for another time when you have access to a stand mixer or, for more delicate tasks, grab a trusty whisk or silicone spatula to do the work.

Don't Forget to Scrape!

A stand mixer usually does a wonderful job of mixing batter, but you still need to do your part too. When scraping down the bowl, be sure to get the sides, bottom, *and* beater to release stuck bits and ensure a uniform texture. Be especially mindful of this at the beginning, when creaming butter and sugar, and at the very end—once you're done mixing, scrape down the bowl and fold the batter a few times to incorporate any butter or egg residue or dry lumps (ideally you won't have any!) so that the batter is smooth and even.

Check Temperature

Set out ingredients that need to be room temperature an hour or two before baking. Cake is essentially a fat-in-liquid emulsion—if one ingredient is colder than another, the batter won't combine properly, resulting in a compromised crumb.

To test if butter is room temperature, press into it with your finger—it should feel slightly cool to the touch (65 to 70 degrees F), and your finger should make an indent but not sink into it. It should feel pliable and appear matte, not shiny or greasy. Cutting butter into cubes and separating it on a plate helps bring it to room temperature more quickly.

Ready the Oven

For all my cakes, I position the oven rack in the center and place the pan in the middle. I have found that it takes a full 30 to 45 minutes for most ovens to properly preheat—and even then, they might be inaccurate. I highly recommend getting an oven thermometer if you want to know what's going on in there. Also, be aware of variables that might affect baking time, such as the following.

CONVECTION OVEN: When using one, reduce the oven temperature by 25 degrees F and start checking your cake for doneness 5 to 10 minutes before the recommended bake time.

DARK PAN: Dark pans absorb and distribute heat more quickly and efficiently. Start checking your cake 5 to 10 minutes before the recommended baking time, especially for Bundt and loaf pans. If you find that the edges of your cake tend to burn in a dark pan, try reducing the oven temperature by 25 degrees F.

Keep an Eye on the Cake

While I've tested these recipes thoroughly to ensure reliable bake times, they're still just recommendations. Because everyone's ovens, stove tops, and equipment are different, go by the visual doneness cues provided and trust your senses.

To Refrigerate or Not

Refrigerate a cake only if it has a perishable filling or frosting. Allow frosting to set in the fridge before loosely, but thoroughly, covering with plastic wrap—if needed, you can also insert toothpicks on the sides and top to keep the wrap from touching the cake. For best taste, allow the cake to sit at room temperature for anywhere from 30 to 90 minutes (depending on ambient temperature) before serving. For cakes that can be kept at room temperature, cover with a cake dome or tightly wrap with plastic wrap or another airtight barrier.

To freeze cake, wrap the cake in plastic wrap twice, then wrap in aluminum foil; it will keep for up to 2 months. Allow to thaw in a refrigerator overnight before frosting or serving (or don't and eat it frozen!).

BAKING TOOLS

Bundt Pan

Look for a sturdy light-colored metal pan—preferably aluminum or coated steel—that will conduct heat evenly and efficiently, won't warp in the oven, and will generously accommodate any Bundt cake recipe (a 12-cup will work for all of the recipes here). The interior should be nonstick to aid in release. A classic fluted pan is the most recognizable Bundt, but these days they come in all sorts of elaborate designs. Nordic Ware is the gold standard. Note that the shape and design of your Bundt pan may affect baking time.

Tube Pan

You'll also want a 10-inch diameter tube pan that, in contrast to a Bundt pan, isn't nonstick. You can use it to bake a pound cake, as well as an angel or chiffon cake. One with a removable bottom and tripod feet is recommended. I love my Chicago Metallic pan.

Round Pan

Most of the round cake recipes in this book call for a 9-inch round pan—having two around is helpful for layer cakes. Since I discovered the 3-inch-deep lightweight anodized and aluminum pans from Fat Daddio's, I've never looked back. They produce a golden, perfectly even, straight-sided cake every time. Because they're so deep, you'll also never have to worry about spillover.

Springform Pans

A 9-inch nonstick springform metal pan with removable sides is important for delicate cakes that can't be removed by flipping them out. Look for ones that are tightly sealed—you don't want a leak in the oven to smoke up your whole kitchen! Hiware makes an excellent one, as does Nordic Ware.

CAKE PANS

A good cake pan can make all the difference, and unfortunately not all are created equal. While pans from the grocery store will work in a pinch, there are others that will produce a much better bake. Whatever the quality, it's important to use the shape and size pan called for in the recipe.

Square and Rectangular Pans	Having both an 8-inch square pan and a 9-by-13-inch pan that are sharp-cornered, light-colored, and aluminized steel is essential—the ones from USA Pan are my pick.
Loaf Pans	I bake with either 8½-by-4½-inch or 9-by-5-inch pans. These cakes come out much thicker than with round and square pans, and as a result take longer to bake and are prone to burned edges. If you're going to invest in one set of good cake pans, I'd do it with this shape. My heavy-gauge aluminized steel pans from USA Pan bake up gorgeous cakes every time.
Quarter- and Half-Sheet Pans	While these aren't typically thought of as cake pans, sheet pans are wonderful when you're aiming to feed a crowd. Having two half-sheet (13-by-18-inch) pans that are light-colored, heavy-duty, and rimmed are also indispensable for toasting nuts, roasting fruits, and the like. Quarter-sheet (9½-by-13-inch) pans are equally useful.
Cast-Iron Skillet	A well-seasoned 10-inch cast-iron skillet makes a great baking vessel, especially when it comes to rustic skillet and upside-down cakes. Make sure you give it a good scrubbing before using it to bake—you don't want last night's dinner permeating your lovely cake!
Glass or Ceramic Baking Dishes	I recommend these in 2- and 3-quart sizes for roasting fruit and baking cakes like the French Custard Cake (page 109) and Golden-Milk Tres Leches Cake (page 111).
Pastry Brush	A soft natural-fiber bristle pastry brush is essential for greasing cake pans and brushing syrups and glazes onto cakes. You can also use a silicone brush.

Parchment Paper	Parchment paper is useful for lining pans, which helps cakes release more easily. Look for unbleached white or natural parchment.
Oven Thermometer	They are inexpensive and essential for baking. The first time I used a thermometer, I was shocked at how long it actually took to properly preheat my oven—and then how many degrees it was off!
Kitchen Scale	A fast and accurate digital scale, like the Escali Primo or Ozeri Pronto, shouldn't set back the home baker more than 25 dollars.
Fine Mesh Sieve	I use a larger one for sifting powdered sugar, cocoa powder, and dry ingredients together; a smaller one for dusting pans and straining freshly squeezed citrus juice.
Rasp Grater	Often referred to as a Microplane, these graters have fine teeth for grating citrus zest and spices. A larger box grater is useful for shredding doughs and vegetables like parsnips, carrots, and zucchini.
Citrus Juicer	You can juice citrus fruits by squeezing them in your hand while trying to catch the seeds, but a citrus juicer is nice to have.
Mortar and Pestle	You'll notice I call for a lot of crushed spices and dried flowers throughout the book. A small marble or granite mortar and pestle (about 1 cup in volume) is perfect for these tasks.
Measuring Cups and Spoons	Measure dry and semisolid ingredients (e.g., yogurt, pumpkin puree, peanut butter) in graduated dry measuring cups. Measure liquids in clear liquid measuring cups, which have a spout for pouring. A spoon set is essential for measuring small quantities, like of salt, leavening, extracts, and spices.

Mixing Bowls	A set of nested metal mixing bowls in various sizes is a must-have. Also, heatproof glass bowls are useful for setting on top of pans with simmering water to melt butter, chocolate, etc.
Stand Mixer	A sturdy stand mixer is a kitchen workhorse. I was gifted my candy-apple-red KitchenAid 5-quart mixer eleven years ago, and it's still serving me well today. If you bake often, consider getting an extra bowl and beater so you don't have to wash between uses. Also, I highly recommend a flex edge beater that scrapes the sides of the bowl while mixing, making the process more efficient. A powerful hand mixer is a decent alternative.
Stainless Steel Whisks	I prefer a balloon whisk for beating egg whites, heavy cream, and other thick ingredients, and a long, narrow whisk for combining batters, stirring, and reaching corners in bowls and pans.
Spatulas	I use heatproof silicone spatulas for folding batters and scraping them into prepared pans, and for use over heat. Offset spatulas are wonderful for decorating and frosting cakes, leveling batter, and for helping with cake removal from a pan.
Digital Instant Thermometer	A thermometer is useful for caramelizing sugar and is also helpful in determining if a cake is done. While I don't count on it as the sole marker, the internal temperature of a fully baked cake should usually be between 200 and 210 degrees F.
Wire Cooling Rack	A large raised rack that is 12 by 17 inches will allow you to set two cakes side by side and will fit inside a half-sheet pan.
Cake Stand and Dome	Cake stands and domes come in a variety of sizes and styles. One that is 9 inches in diameter will fit most cakes in this book.

BAKING INGREDIENTS

Flour

The recipes in this book were tested with Gold Medal bleached all-purpose flour (unbleached is fine too). Cake, spelt, rye, almond, and hazelnut flours are also occasionally used.

Sweeteners

Granulated sugar is called for most frequently, as well as light and dark brown sugar, powdered sugar, and turbinado sugar. Some cakes also use molasses, honey, maple syrup, and maple sugar.

Butter and Oils

I prefer unsalted butter because it gives me more control of how much salt is in my baked goods. If you only have salted butter on hand, reduce the overall amount of salt in the recipe to ¼ teaspoon per ½ cup (115 g) butter. Many of my cakes rely on oil as well—the ones I use most are canola, safflower, coconut, and olive oil.

Eggs

Eggs should be large and usually at room temperature. If you forget to set out your eggs in advance, put them in a bowl and cover with hot tap water—after 10 minutes they'll be ready to go.

Dairy Products

Whole milk was used when testing the recipes. I recommend Philadelphia brand cream cheese for its flavor and texture. For other dairy products, such as buttermilk, heavy cream, sour cream, whole-milk ricotta, and mascarpone, use the best quality you can find.

Salt

I always use Diamond Crystal kosher salt because it's lighter and less salty than other kosher or sea salts. If you don't have this brand, a fine sea salt is a good alternative, but start by halving the amount of salt the recipe calls for. Remember, you can always add, but you can never take away. I use flaky sea salt for finishing—Maldon or Jacobsen Salt Co. are excellent choices.

Leavening Agents

Baking soda and baking powder lose leavening power over time—try to replace them every six months or so. To check freshness, place 1 teaspoon in a small bowl and pour boiling water on top—if they fizz, they're still good.

Cocoa Powder and Chocolate

I use both unsweetened natural and Dutch-process cocoa powder in this book. Do buy the highest-fat (22 to 24 percent) cocoa available—it makes a world of a difference in baked goods.

As for chocolate, semisweet (around 60 percent) or bittersweet (around 70 percent) will work well and are interchangeable depending on what you have on hand and how bitter you want the resulting cake to be. If using milk chocolate, be sure it's good quality.

Vanilla

I use pure vanilla extract in almost all my recipes. Vanilla bean paste is a cost-effective alternative to whole beans for when you want that bean-flecked visual cue, such as in pastry cream.

Fresh Spices

For best flavor, buy loose spices in small quantities from a reputable spice shop or the bulk section of grocery stores that have high turnover.

Nuts and Seeds

As with spices, buy nuts and seeds from the bulk section of grocery stores that have high turnover. Store in an airtight container in a cool, dark place if they will be used quickly, or in the freezer for up to a year or more to keep them from going rancid.

Flowers

I love using flowers such as hibiscus, rose, orange blossom, and lavender in my baking. If you can't find them dried in the bulk spice section, a spice shop is a good next stop. Rose water and orange blossom water can be found in the baking aisle or with the Middle Eastern or Indian foods in a well-stocked grocery store.

Bundt and Tube Cakes

GETTING BUNDT CAKES RIGHT

The tricky part about Bundts is that removal from the pan can be a bit spotty—but it doesn't have to be. After baking dozens of Bundt cakes, here are my tips for a beautiful release:

Choose the Right Pan

Nordic Ware is credited with originating this pan shape, and luckily for us, they still make the best on the market. See page 8 for more information.

Grease the Pan

My preference is to grease Bundt pans with either nonstick spray, oil, or melted shortening. Butter, unlike the other three, contains water and milk solids that will cause spots where the batter might stick—a no-no here. I like to use a pastry brush to evenly and thoroughly coat every pan nook and cranny with fat, even when working with nonstick spray.

Dust the Pan

Flour, or in some cases cocoa, locks the batter in to create an even, browned crust that helps prevent the cake from sticking. Work over the sink and use a sieve to generously dust the inside walls and the center tube. Hold the pan on its side and slowly rotate it, tapping it against the counter with each turn to dislodge excess flour and coat any unfloured spots. Continue turning and tapping until the pan is evenly coated. Flip the pan upside down and tap it against the rim of the sink to remove any excess flour. The pan is now ready to be filled!

Remove from the Pan

The best time to invert and release the cake is when it's cooled just enough to set yet still warm enough that it will slip right out. After the cake has cooled for 15 minutes in the pan, insert a small offset spatula or butter knife between the edge of the pan and cake and use it to gently pull the cake away from the sides of the pan. Invert a wire rack on top and, using oven mitts to protect your hands, quickly flip the whole thing over. The cake should ideally slip right out. Let the cake sit for a few minutes before tapping the wire rack against the counter to free the cake from the pan. Lift the pan and let the cake cool completely.

RHUBARB BUTTERMILK BUNDT CAKE

3¼ cups (420 g) all-purpose flour, plus more for dusting
1 tablespoon baking powder
1½ teaspoons kosher salt
3 eggs, at room temperature
2 egg yolks, at room temperature
1 tablespoon vanilla extract
1 tablespoon finely grated lemon or orange zest
2 cups (400 g) granulated sugar
1 cup (225 g) unsalted butter, at room temperature
1 cup (240 ml) buttermilk, at room temperature
12 ounces (340 g) rhubarb, trimmed and cut into ¼-inch-thick slices (3 cups)

For the glaze
1¾ cups (210 g) powdered sugar
3 to 4 tablespoons freshly squeezed lemon or orange juice, strained
½ teaspoon vanilla extract

You either love or hate rhubarb, and if there's something I've learned about the Pacific Northwest since moving to Seattle, it's that people *love* it here. Even without the rhubarb, this Bundt is a good one—a few extra egg yolks keep the cake tender while acidic buttermilk helps soften and enrich the crumb and adds a slight tangy edge. Use the cake to spotlight other fruit when rhubarb isn't in season, and instead of citrus, play around with spices or flower essences like rose water and orange blossom. If your stalks are thick, halve them lengthwise before slicing.

MAKES 8 TO 10 SERVINGS

• Preheat the oven to 350 degrees F. Lightly but evenly grease a 12- to 15-cup Bundt pan and dust the inside with flour (see page 21).

• In a medium bowl, whisk together the flour, baking powder, and salt. In a small bowl, whisk together the eggs, egg yolks, and vanilla.

• In the bowl of a stand mixer fitted with the paddle attachment, use your fingers to rub the zest into the sugar until it has taken on the citrus color and perfume. Add the butter and beat on medium speed until light and fluffy, 4 to 5 minutes, scraping down the bottom and sides of the bowl often. Reduce the speed to medium-low and gradually add the egg mixture a bit at a time, letting it fully incorporate before adding more and scraping down the bowl as needed.

• Reduce the speed to low and add the flour mixture to the batter in three additions, alternating with three additions of the buttermilk, mixing until just combined and scraping down the bowl as needed. The batter should be thick and smooth (see Note). Use a silicone spatula to gently fold in the rhubarb slices by hand.

• Scrape the batter into the prepared pan and smooth out the top. Bake until the cake is golden, looks set, and a tester inserted into the center comes out clean, 55 to 65 minutes. Remove the cake from the oven and let it cool for about 15 minutes before inverting and releasing it onto a wire rack (see page 21). Allow the cake to cool completely.

• To make the glaze, in a medium bowl, stir together the powdered sugar, 3 tablespoons citrus juice, and vanilla until smooth. Use the back of a spoon to work the glaze against the side of the bowl to remove any clumps. The glaze should be thick but pourable. If it seems too stiff, add more juice 1 teaspoon at a time.

• Transfer the cooled cake to a serving plate. Pour the glaze evenly over the top and let it set for 20 minutes before serving. This cake keeps well wrapped at room temperature for 3 to 4 days.

SOUR CREAM COFFEE CAKE WITH FIVE-SPICE STREUSEL

For the streusel

¾ cup (100 g) all-purpose flour
⅓ cup (65 g) packed light brown sugar
¼ cup (50 g) granulated sugar
2 teaspoons five-spice powder
1½ teaspoons ground cinnamon
½ teaspoon kosher salt
1 cup (115 g) toasted pecans, finely chopped
5 tablespoons (70 g) unsalted butter, melted

For the filling

1 cup (115 g) toasted pecans, finely chopped
¼ cup (50 g) packed light brown sugar
¾ teaspoon five-spice powder
½ teaspoon ground cinnamon
Pinch of kosher salt

This coffee cake has all the makings of my platonic ideal: rich sour cream cake, thick swirls of spiced brown sugar, and a nut-studded, buttery streusel that ties it all together. For extra oomph, I've also added five-spice powder to the mix. The blend features two familiar spices, cinnamon and cloves, along with star anise, fennel, and Szechuan peppercorns. The cake's bold, complex flavor will leave anyone taking a bite delightfully surprised. Serve it at your next brunch or snack on it during the week when nothing but a piece of cake will do.

MAKES 10 TO 12 SERVINGS

◆ Preheat the oven to 350 degrees F. Lightly but evenly grease a 10-inch tube pan and dust the inside with flour (see page 21).

◆ To make the streusel, in a medium bowl, whisk together the flour, both sugars, five-spice, cinnamon, and salt. Stir in the pecans and melted butter and mix to combine. The topping should form crumbs and hold together when pinched. Chill in the freezer.

◆ To make the filling, in a small bowl, whisk together the pecans, sugar, five-spice, cinnamon, and salt.

◆ To make the cake, in a medium bowl, whisk together the flour, baking powder, salt, and baking soda.

For the cake
2⅔ cups (345 g) all-purpose flour, plus more for dusting
2 teaspoons baking powder
1 teaspoon kosher salt
½ teaspoon baking soda
1½ cups (300 g) granulated sugar
¾ cup (170 g) unsalted butter, at room temperature
4 eggs, at room temperature
1 tablespoon vanilla extract
1½ cups (360 g) sour cream, at room temperature

◆ In the bowl of a stand mixer fitted with the paddle attachment, beat the sugar and butter on medium speed until light and fluffy, 4 to 5 minutes, scraping down the bottom and sides of the bowl often. Reduce the speed to medium-low and add the eggs one a time, beating to fully incorporate after each addition and scraping down the bowl as needed. Add the vanilla and mix to combine.

◆ Reduce the speed to low and add the flour mixture in three additions, alternating with two additions of sour cream, mixing until just combined and scraping down the bowl as needed. The batter will be thick and smooth.

◆ Pour one-third of the batter into the prepared pan. Smooth out the top and sprinkle evenly with half of the filling mixture. Repeat with another third of the batter and the remaining filling. Top with the remaining batter and sprinkle with an even layer of the streusel.

◆ Bake until a tester inserted in the center of the cake comes out clean, 50 to 60 minutes. Transfer the pan to a wire rack and allow the cake to cool completely.

◆ When cooled, run a knife or offset spatula around the sides of the pan and push the cake up and out from the bottom. Slide the spatula between the bottom of the cake and the pan to loosen it, and flip the cake, ideally over a sink, onto a large plate. Invert again onto a serving plate and serve. This cake keeps well wrapped at room temperature for 4 to 5 days.

MAMA'S RUM RAISIN BUNDT CAKE

2¼ cups *minus* 1 tablespoon (285 g) all-purpose flour, plus more for dusting
1½ cups (300 g) granulated sugar
1 (3.4-ounce) box French vanilla or vanilla instant pudding mix
2 teaspoons baking powder
1¼ teaspoons kosher salt
4 eggs, at room temperature
½ cup (120 ml) whole milk, at room temperature
½ cup (120 ml) light or dark rum
¼ cup (60 ml) vegetable oil
2 teaspoons vanilla extract
¾ cup (170 g) unsalted butter, cubed, at room temperature
¾ cup (115 g) golden raisins
¾ cup (85 g) toasted walnuts, chopped (optional)

This is my mom's signature cake for potlucks and church gatherings. With almost a whole cup of rum in the ingredient list, you would think her fellow churchgoers would abstain from a slice. But it's always the first dessert to go, its boozy flavor the main draw. Her recipe, snipped from a Bacardi rum ad, calls for boxed cake mix (which I ditched) and instant pudding (which I kept). My mostly from-scratch version, like the original, results in a velvety crumb that's studded with raisins and walnuts. The butter-rum glaze soaks through the cake from the bottom and the top, leaving it ultra-moist and irresistible. If extra glaze is enticing, feel free to double it.

MAKES 8 TO 10 SERVINGS

◆ Preheat the oven to 325 degrees F. Lightly but evenly grease a 10- to 12-cup Bundt pan and dust the inside with flour (see page 21).

◆ In the bowl of a stand mixer, whisk together by hand the flour, sugar, pudding mix, baking powder, and salt. In a medium bowl, use the same whisk to combine the eggs, milk, rum, oil, and vanilla until smooth.

◆ Add the butter to the dry ingredients. Fit the mixer with the paddle attachment and beat on low speed until the butter is incorporated and the mixture resembles coarse sand with no visible chunks, 2 to 3 minutes.

◆ Pour in half of the egg mixture and beat on low speed until the flour mixture is hydrated. Stop the mixer, scrape down the bottom and sides of the bowl, and pour in the remaining

For the glaze
½ cup (100 g) granulated sugar
¼ cup (55 g) unsalted butter
2 tablespoons water
¼ cup (60 ml) light or dark rum
½ teaspoon vanilla extract

egg mixture. Beat on low speed until fully incorporated. The batter will be thin and runny at this point. Scrape down the bowl, then slowly increase the speed to medium and beat for 1 minute. Pause to scrape the bowl again, then beat for another 30 seconds—the batter will be smooth, pale in color, and very thick. Stir in the raisins and walnuts by hand to incorporate.

◆ Scrape the batter into the prepared pan and smooth out the top. Bake until the cake is golden, looks set, and a tester inserted into the center comes out clean, 55 to 70 minutes. Remove the cake from the oven and allow to slightly cool.

◆ While the cake is baking, make the glaze. In a small saucepan, combine the sugar, butter, and water. Bring to a boil over medium-high heat, then reduce to a simmer. Cook, without stirring, for 5 to 7 minutes, or until the syrup thickens slightly. Remove from the heat and stir in the rum and vanilla.

◆ Poke holes all over the top of the warm cake with a wooden skewer or chopstick. Gradually pour three-quarters of the glaze over the cake, allowing it to absorb the glaze before adding more. Allow the cake to cool for 15 to 20 minutes before inverting and releasing it onto a wire rack (see page 21). Brush with the remaining glaze; if it has thickened, simply rewarm over low heat.

◆ Allow the cake to completely cool before transferring to a serving plate. This cake is best the next day and gets better with age; it keeps well wrapped at room temperature for up to 5 days.

DOUBLE-CHOCOLATE ZUCCHINI BUNDT CAKE

¼ cup (25 g) Dutch-process cocoa powder, plus more for dusting
2 cups (260 g) all-purpose flour
1½ teaspoons instant espresso powder
1¼ teaspoons kosher salt
1 teaspoon baking powder
¾ teaspoon baking soda
3 eggs, at room temperature
1½ cups (300 g) packed light brown sugar
1 cup (235 ml) neutral oil, such as canola or safflower
1½ teaspoons vanilla extract
1½ ounces (45 g) unsweetened chocolate, melted and slightly cooled
2½ cups (325 g) lightly packed grated or shredded unpeeled zucchini

For the ganache
4 ounces (115 g) semisweet or bittersweet chocolate, finely chopped
½ cup (120 ml) heavy cream
1 tablespoon light corn syrup (optional)
½ teaspoon vanilla extract
Pinch of kosher salt

Zucchini is the star of this Bundt for the way it locks in the cake's moisture for days. Look for small to medium-size squash; the supersize ones tend to be dry and bitter and have large, tough seeds. The addition of chocolate both in the batter and glaze turns this unassuming cake into one of those "one more piece" desserts. Using corn syrup results in a glossy chocolate ganache glaze that keeps its shine, but feel free to omit it if desired.

MAKES 8 TO 10 SERVINGS

◆ Preheat the oven to 350 degrees F. Lightly but evenly grease a 10- to 12-cup Bundt pan and dust the inside with cocoa powder (see page 21).

◆ In a medium bowl, sift together the flour, cocoa powder, espresso powder, salt, baking powder, and baking soda, and whisk to combine. In a large bowl, whisk together the eggs, sugar, oil, and vanilla. Use your fingers or the back of a spoon to break up any sugar clumps. Whisk the cooled melted chocolate into the egg mixture and then the zucchini. Using a silicone spatula, fold in the flour mixture until it is fully incorporated and a thick batter forms—try to not mix more than necessary.

◆ Scrape the batter into the prepared pan. Bake until the cake is matte, looks set, and a tester inserted into the center comes out clean, 45 to 55 minutes. Remove the cake from the oven and let it cool for about 15 minutes before inverting and releasing it onto a wire rack (see page 21). Allow the cake to cool completely. ⟶

◆ To make the ganache, place the chocolate in a small bowl. In a small saucepan over medium-low heat, while stirring to combine, bring the cream and corn syrup to a simmer. Pour the mixture over the chocolate and let it sit, undisturbed, for 1 minute. Gently whisk until smooth. Stir in the vanilla and salt. Cool until slightly thickened, about 10 minutes. The ganache will keep for up to 1 week in the refrigerator—rewarm before using.

◆ Transfer the cooled cake to a wire rack set over a parchment paper–lined baking sheet, then slowly pour or drizzle the ganache evenly over the top, allowing it to drip down the sides. Let it set for 30 to 60 minutes before serving. This cake keeps well wrapped at room temperature for 3 to 4 days.

SUGARED JELLY DONUT BUNDT CAKE

3 cups (390 g) all-purpose
  flour, plus more for dusting
1 tablespoon baking powder
1½ teaspoons lightly packed
  freshly grated nutmeg
1½ teaspoons kosher salt
¼ teaspoon baking soda
½ cup (120 ml) whole milk, at
  room temperature
½ cup (120 g) sour cream, at
  room temperature
¾ cup (250 g) fruit jelly,
  jam, or preserves, at room
  temperature
1 cup (225 g) unsalted butter,
  at room temperature
1 cup (200 g) granulated sugar
½ cup (100 g) packed light
  brown sugar
4 eggs, at room temperature

For the spiced-sugar coating
½ cup (100 g) granulated sugar
1 teaspoon ground cinnamon
½ teaspoon lightly packed
  freshly grated nutmeg
¼ cup (55 g) unsalted butter,
  melted

With a ripple of jelly, a generous grating of fresh nutmeg, and a coating of melted butter and spiced sugar, this cake is essentially a donut in Bundt form and one of my favorite breakfast cakes. The golden exterior turns slightly crisp as it cools, while the crumb stays soft and tender, just like the old-fashioned treat. Delicious on the day it's baked, it gets even better with age. Play around with the preserves, using whatever is in season or on hand—you can't go wrong!

MAKES 8 TO 10 SERVINGS

◆ Preheat the oven to 350 degrees F. Lightly but evenly grease a 12- to 15-cup Bundt pan and dust the inside with flour (see page 21).

◆ In a medium bowl, whisk together the flour, baking powder, nutmeg, salt, and baking soda. In a small bowl, whisk together the milk and sour cream. In another medium bowl, measure out the jelly.

◆ In the bowl of a stand mixer fitted with the paddle attachment, beat the butter and both sugars on medium speed until light and fluffy, 4 to 5 minutes, scraping down the bottom and sides often. Reduce the speed to medium-low and add the eggs one at a time, beating to fully incorporate after each addition and scraping down the bowl as needed. ⟶

* Reduce the speed to low and add the flour mixture in three additions, alternating with three additions of the milk mixture, mixing until just combined and scraping down the bowl as needed. The batter should be thick and smooth.

* Stir a generous 1 cup (about 250 g) of the batter into the jelly to thoroughly combine. Scrape two-thirds of the plain batter into the prepared pan and top it with an even layer of the jelly batter. Dollop the remaining plain batter evenly on top, and use an offset spatula or the back of a spoon to carefully smooth it out. Work a skewer or chopstick through the batter in a wavy motion to swirl the layers together.

* Bake until the cake is golden, looks set, and a tester inserted into the center comes out clean, 45 to 55 minutes. Remove the cake from the oven and let it cool for about 20 minutes before inverting and releasing it onto a wire rack (see page 21). Place the rack with the cake over a parchment-lined baking sheet.

* While the cake is cooling, make the spiced-sugar coating. In a small bowl, combine the sugar, cinnamon, and nutmeg. Brush the warm cake evenly with the melted butter. Sprinkle the top with the spiced sugar, then use your fingers to lightly rub it onto the sides to help it stick. Continue until the whole cake is coated in spiced sugar, as if it were a giant donut.

* Allow the cake to cool completely before serving. It keeps well wrapped at room temperature for 3 to 4 days.

GRAPEFRUIT POPPY SEED CAKE WITH HIBISCUS GLAZE

3 cups (390 g) all-purpose flour, plus more for dusting

⅓ cup (50 g) poppy seeds, plus more for optional garnish

1½ teaspoons baking powder

1½ teaspoons kosher salt

¾ teaspoon baking soda

2 tablespoons finely grated grapefruit zest (from 1 large grapefruit)

2 teaspoons finely grated lemon zest (from 1 medium lemon)

1½ cups (300 g) granulated sugar

¾ cup (170 g) unsalted butter, at room temperature

4 eggs, at room temperature

2 teaspoons vanilla extract

1½ cups (360 g) sour cream, at room temperature

For the citrus syrup

½ cup (100 g) granulated sugar

⅓ cup (80 ml) freshly squeezed grapefruit juice, strained (from ½ large grapefruit)

3 tablespoons freshly squeezed lemon juice, strained

CONTINUED

This Bundt is inspired by one at Coyle's Bakeshop, one of my favorite bakeries in Seattle. The poppy seed–studded cake is first soaked with a grapefruit-lemon syrup and then finished with a hibiscus glaze for an extra pop of color and tartness. On the day it's baked, the texture is airy and cotton-like, but as it sits, the syrup soaks through the crumb—not only infusing it with flavor, but also keeping it incredibly moist.

MAKES 8 TO 10 SERVINGS

◆ Preheat the oven to 350 degrees F. Lightly but evenly grease a 10- to 12-cup Bundt pan and dust the inside with flour (see page 21).

◆ In a medium bowl, whisk together the flour, poppy seeds, baking powder, salt, and baking soda.

◆ In the bowl of a stand mixer fitted with the paddle attachment, use your fingers to rub the zests into the sugar until it has taken on the citrus color and perfume. Add the butter and beat on medium speed until light and fluffy, 4 to 5 minutes, scraping down the bottom and sides of the bowl often. Reduce the speed to medium-low and add the eggs one at a time, beating to fully incorporate after each addition and scraping down the bowl as needed. Add the vanilla and mix to combine.

◆ Reduce the speed to low and add the flour mixture to the batter in three additions, alternating with two additions of the sour cream, mixing until just combined and scraping down the bowl as needed. ⟶

For the hibiscus glaze
1¾ cups (180 g) powdered
sugar
3 to 4 tablespoons freshly
squeezed grapefruit juice,
strained
2 teaspoons crushed or
ground dried hibiscus
flowers

NOTE: You can buy hibis-
cus flowers either loose
(usually in the bulk tea or
spice section) or in tea bags
(you'll need the contents
of 2 to 3 satchels). Crush
the flowers in a mortar and
pestle until finely ground,
or use a spice grinder to
process them. Because the
tangy hibiscus glaze turns
a bright fuchsia color the
longer it sits, you can make
it a few hours beforehand
for a beautiful effect.

◆ Scrape the batter into the prepared pan and smooth out
the top. Bake until the cake is starting to brown, looks set,
and a tester inserted into the center comes out clean, 45 to
55 minutes. Remove the cake from the oven and allow it to
cool slightly.

◆ Meanwhile, make the citrus syrup. In a small saucepan over
low heat, stir together the sugar and citrus juices until the
sugar has dissolved.

◆ Poke holes all over the top of the warm cake with a wooden
skewer or chopstick. Gradually pour half of the syrup over
the cake, allowing it absorb the syrup before adding more.
Allow the cake to cool for 15 to 20 minutes before inverting
and releasing it onto a wire rack (see page 21). Brush with the
remaining syrup. Allow the cake to cool completely.

◆ To make the hibiscus glaze, in a medium bowl, stir together
the powdered sugar, 3 tablespoons grapefruit juice, and hibiscus until smooth. Use the back of a spoon to work the mixture
against the side of the bowl to remove any clumps. The glaze
should be thick but pourable. If it seems too stiff, add more
juice 1 teaspoon at a time.

◆ Transfer the cooled cake to a serving plate. Pour the glaze
evenly over the top and garnish with a sprinkle of poppy
seeds. Let it set for 20 minutes before serving. This cake keeps
well wrapped at room temperature for 3 to 4 days.

GINGERBREAD BUNDT CAKE WITH LEMON MASCARPONE ICING

2⅓ cups (305 g) all-purpose flour, plus more for dusting
1 tablespoon ground ginger
1½ teaspoons ground cinnamon
1¼ teaspoons kosher salt
1 teaspoon baking soda
¾ teaspoon freshly ground black pepper
½ teaspoon ground cloves
½ teaspoon lightly packed freshly grated nutmeg
1½ cups (300 g) packed light brown sugar
3 eggs, at room temperature
½ cup (190 g) mild molasses (see Note)
1 tablespoon finely grated peeled fresh ginger
1½ teaspoons vanilla extract
¾ cup (175 ml) neutral oil, such as canola or safflower
¾ cup (175 ml) buttermilk, at room temperature
¼ cup (40 g) crystallized ginger, finely chopped, for topping

CONTINUED

This gingerbread bakes up big, bold, and positively scrumptious. Fresh and ground ginger, black pepper, and a generous dose of other spices deliver a punch of flavor, meanwhile a measured pour of molasses and buttermilk leave the cake soft but not too sticky or dense. For the holidays, I love to adorn it with a bright lemon mascarpone icing and a crown of crystallized ginger but know it's equally good without the accessories.

MAKES 8 TO 10 SERVINGS

◆ Preheat the oven to 350 degrees F. Lightly but evenly grease a 10- to 12-cup Bundt pan and dust the inside with flour (see page 21).

◆ In a medium bowl, whisk together the flour, ginger, cinnamon, salt, baking soda, pepper, cloves, and nutmeg.

◆ In the bowl of a stand mixer fitted with the whisk attachment mix the brown sugar and eggs on medium-high speed until thick ribbons form (see page 42), 8 to 10 minutes. Reduce the speed to medium-low and gradually pour in the molasses, scraping down the bottom and sides of the bowl as needed, followed by the fresh ginger and vanilla. Beat for another minute. With the mixer running, gradually pour in the oil and mix until fully incorporated. ⟶

For the icing

½ cup (115 g) mascarpone cheese

1½ ounces (45 g) cream cheese, at room temperature

½ cup (60 g) powdered sugar

1½ teaspoons finely grated lemon zest (from 1 small lemon)

1 teaspoon freshly squeezed lemon juice

½ teaspoon vanilla extract

Pinch of kosher salt

2 to 4 tablespoons heavy cream

NOTE: Blackstrap molasses overpowers the flavors of this sweet cake, so be sure to use an unsulphured mild one, like Grandma's brand.

• Add the flour mixture in three additions, mixing until just combined and scraping down the bowl as needed. With the mixer running, gradually pour in the buttermilk until just incorporated. Scrape down the bowl and use a silicone spatula to fold the batter a few times to make sure it's smooth.

• Scrape the batter into the prepared pan. Bake the cake until it feels firm and springs back when pressed and a tester inserted in the center comes out clean, 45 to 55 minutes. Remove the cake from the oven and let it cool for about 15 minutes before inverting and releasing it onto a wire rack (see page 21). Allow the cake to cool completely.

• To make the icing, in the bowl of a stand mixer fitted with the paddle attachment, beat the mascarpone and cream cheese on medium speed until smooth, scraping down the bowl as needed. Sift in the powdered sugar, then add the lemon zest and juice, vanilla, and salt. Beat on medium speed until smooth. Mix in 2 tablespoons heavy cream—the icing should be thick but pourable. If it seems too stiff, add more cream 1 teaspoon at a time.

• Transfer the cooled cake to a serving plate. Spoon the icing over the top of the cake, tapping the plate to encourage the icing to run down the sides. Top with the crystallized ginger and serve. This cake keeps well wrapped in the refrigerator for 3 or 4 days.

THE RIBBON STAGE

The ribbon stage refers to the foam-like batter created when eggs and sugar are beaten together. When you lift the whisk out, thick ribbons will drizzle off and sit on top of the batter for a few seconds before dissolving. The batter is usually very thick, pale in color, and roughly tripled in volume at this point.

RASPBERRY-ROSE ANGEL FOOD CAKE

⅔ cup (80 g) powdered sugar
½ cup (60 g) cake flour
½ teaspoon kosher salt
¾ cup (190 g) egg whites
(from 5 to 6 eggs), at room
temperature
¾ teaspoon cream of tartar
½ cup (100 g) granulated
sugar, divided
1 teaspoon rose water
½ teaspoon vanilla extract

For the whipped cream
2 cups (475 ml) cold heavy
cream
¼ cup (30 g) powdered sugar
¾ teaspoon rose water
¼ teaspoon kosher salt

For assembly
1½ cups (6.5 ounces) fresh
raspberries
2 tablespoons roasted
shelled pistachios, whole or
crushed, for garnish
Dried rose petals, for garnish

A full-size angel food cake can call for up to a carton of eggs, but this half-dozen version is much more approachable and still makes plenty to go around. The key to these cloudlike cakes is whipped egg whites and zero fat, resulting in a uniquely light, airy, and slightly chewy texture. This sweet take features a delicate rose-scented cake filled with fresh raspberries and whipped cream—a garnish of pistachios and dried rose petals hint at the flavors within.

If your tube pan doesn't have legs, you can invert it and insert the long neck of a bottle through the center hole of the pan, or set it on a trio of cans once it comes out of the oven (make sure you have them ready to go!). You'll want to factor in cooling time (around 2 hours) when planning to bake this cake.

MAKES 8 TO 10 SERVINGS

+ Preheat the oven to 350 degrees F.

+ In a medium bowl, measure out the powdered sugar and flour, then sift them together into another medium bowl. Sift two more times. Whisk in the salt.

+ In the bowl of a stand mixer fitted with the whisk attachment, whip the egg whites on low speed for 1 minute to loosen them up. Increase the speed to medium-low and whip until there is no longer a cloudy, yellowish liquid at the bottom, and a white foam forms with large bubbles, 2 to 3 minutes. Add the cream of tartar and whip to incorporate. ⟶

• Increase the speed to medium and keep whipping until the egg whites resemble a thick, dense foam. Gradually add the granulated sugar 1 tablespoon at a time. Continue to beat until the whites are glossy and opaque and soft peaks form (see page 51), 1 to 2 minutes. Add the rose water and vanilla, and mix to incorporate.

• Sprinkle a quarter of the flour mixture over the whites and use a silicone spatula to gently but confidently fold it in by hand, starting from the bottom and folding through the center to ensure no flour remains. Repeat with the remaining flour mixture in three more batches.

• Scrape the batter into an ungreased 10-inch tube pan and work an offset spatula or butter knife through the batter in a zigzag motion one or two times to remove any air pockets. Smooth out the top. Bake until the top is puffed, browned, and springs back when gently pressed, 20 to 25 minutes. Remove the pan from the oven and immediately turn it upside down onto its feet or over a bottle or cans. Allow the cake to cool completely before proceeding.

• Flip the pan right side up and run a paring knife around the outer edge until the cake releases from the sides. Push the cake up and out from the bottom. Run the knife between the bottom of the cake and the pan to loosen it, then flip onto a cutting board. Gently pull on the sides of the cake to release it from the center tube.

• When ready to assemble, make the rose whipped cream. In the bowl of a stand mixer fitted with the whisk attachment, combine the cream, sugar, rose water, and salt. On medium speed, whip the cream until it has thickened and firm peaks form.

• To assemble the cake, first cut it in half crosswise with a serrated knife using a gentle sawing motion. Place the bottom layer (cut side up) onto a cake stand or serving plate. Tuck strips of parchment paper under the edge of the cake to keep the plate clean.

• Arrange the raspberries over the top of the cake in an even layer. Dollop about 1½ cups (355 ml) whipped cream over the raspberries and use an offset spatula to evenly smooth the top. Top with the other cake layer (cut side down). Spread the remaining whipped cream over the top and sides, making swoops and swirls with the spatula or a spoon. Chill for at least 1 hour and up to 6 hours.

• Before serving, sprinkle the cake with pistachios and rose petals. Cut the cake with a serrated knife using a gentle sawing motion. Covered and refrigerated, the cake will keep for up to 2 days.

A PRIMER ON EGG WHITES

- Eggs separate best when cold—the yolks are still firm and less likely to break, and the whites hold together better.

- Even the tiniest trace of fat or egg yolk will interfere with egg whites whipping. To avoid ruining a whole batch, first separate each egg over a small bowl to make sure there is no egg yolk in the white before adding it to the rest of the whites.

- Use a glass, metal, or copper bowl (plastic tends to harbor grease) for whipping, and make sure both the bowl and the whisk are very clean and dry.

- Let the egg whites come to room temperature—this ensures that they whip to their fullest potential.

- I whip egg whites in stages, starting out at a low speed and slowly increasing to medium. The gradual speed adjustment will produce a more stable product.

- These are the four main stages of whipped egg whites:

  FOAMY: Large, very loose bubbles with a cloudy yellowish liquid at the bottom that will develop into bubbles the longer you whip the whites. This is the ideal stage to add cream of tartar or lemon juice.

  SOFT: The bubbles have tightened into a dense white foam. When lifting the whisk out of the whites and turning it upright, the whites will form a soft, droopy peak (pictured on left). This is the ideal stage to start adding sugar if called for.

  FIRM: The foam is glossy, firm, and smooth. When lifting the whisk out of the whites, the peak will have only a slight droop.

  STIFF: The foam is glossy and very stiff. When lifting the whisk out of the whites, the peak will stand up straight.

- Because the stable foam doesn't hold up for very long, use whipped whites or meringue as soon as possible.

PEAR-WALNUT CAKE WITH SPELT AND CARDAMOM

2 cups (260 g) all-purpose flour, plus more for dusting

1 cup (120 g) spelt flour

1½ teaspoons kosher salt

1½ teaspoons finely crushed cardamom seeds, or 1 teaspoon ground cardamom

1 teaspoon baking soda

1½ cups (355 ml) neutral oil, such as canola or safflower

¾ cup (150 g) granulated sugar

¾ cup (150 g) packed light brown sugar

3 eggs, at room temperature

2 teaspoons vanilla extract

2 large ripe but firm pears, peeled, cored, and cut into ¼-inch-thick slices (3 cups or 440 g)

1½ cups (170 g) toasted walnuts, chopped

2 to 3 tablespoons turbinado sugar, for sprinkling (optional)

I, along with many others, have been making some version of Teddie's Apple Cake, originally published in the *New York Times* in 1973, for years. It's easy to throw together, and the oil-based batter produces a toothsome crumb that lets the mix-ins shine. I had a brief stint baking breakfast cakes for a local Seattle company, and I used Teddie's recipe (whoever he may be!) as the springboard for this homey pear cake. It's a big one, but I find there's never any issue with finishing it. When baking with pears, reach for Anjou, Bartlett, or Bosc varieties.

MAKES 10 TO 12 SERVINGS

◆ Preheat the oven to 350 degrees F. Lightly but evenly grease a 10-inch tube pan and dust the inside with flour (see page 21).

◆ In a medium bowl, whisk together the flours, salt, cardamom, and baking soda.

◆ In the bowl of a stand mixer fitted with the paddle attachment, beat the oil and both sugars on medium speed until combined, 4 to 5 minutes. Add the eggs one at a time, beating to fully incorporate after each addition and scraping down the bottom and sides of the bowl as needed. The batter will be creamy. Mix in the vanilla.

◆ Reduce the speed to low and add the flour mixture, mixing until just combined. Use a silicone spatula to gently fold in the pears and walnuts to evenly incorporate.

◆ Scrape the batter into the prepared pan and smooth out the top. Sprinkle it all over with turbinado sugar. Bake for 60 to 70 minutes, or until a tester inserted into the center comes out clean. Remove the pan from the oven and allow the cake to cool completely on a cooling rack before unmolding to serve. This cake keeps well wrapped at room temperature for 3 to 4 days.

VARIATION: Feel free to substitute the spelt flour, which adds a nutty, whole grain note, with another flour, like rye or whole wheat; the cardamom with ground ginger or any combination of warm spices; and the walnuts with hazelnuts or almonds.

HOW TO CRUSH CARDAMOM

To crush cardamom seeds, place whole cardamom pods in a mortar bowl and pound on them with a pestle. Pry open the cracked pods, pick out the seeds within, and discard the outer shell. Continue to pound and crush the seeds with the pestle to grind as finely as possible.

Round
Cakes

BARELY BAKED DULCE DE LECHE CHEESECAKE

For the crust
1¾ cups (195 g) graham cracker crumbs (12 to 13 crackers)
6½ tablespoons (92 g) unsalted butter, melted
¼ cup (50 g) packed light brown sugar
¼ teaspoon kosher salt
¼ teaspoon ground cinnamon

For the filling
1 cup (235 ml) cold heavy cream
¼ cup plus 1 tablespoon (30 g) powdered sugar
13 ounces (385 g) cream cheese, at room temperature
½ cup (140 g) dulce de leche (see Note)
1½ teaspoons vanilla extract
Generous pinch or two of kosher salt

For the topping
½ cup (140 g) dulce de leche
1½ tablespoons heavy cream or whole milk
Flaky sea salt, for sprinkling

Lighter and more mousse-like than its traditional counterpart, this "barely baked" cheesecake relies on whipped cream instead of eggs for structure and stability. Dulce de leche—in the filling and glaze—brings deep buttery, caramelly notes. The only time you'll have to turn on your oven is to bake the crust, which adds depth of flavor. If you want to avoid this step, skip it, but increase the butter to ½ cup (115 g) and freeze the crust for the allotted time. To ensure the filling sets, give it plenty of time to chill (ideally overnight) and use a very thick dulce de leche.

MAKES 8 TO 10 SERVINGS

◆ Preheat the oven to 350 degrees F. Flip the bottom of a 9-inch springform pan upside down so that the lip faces downward (this makes serving much easier). Assemble and lightly grease the pan.

◆ To make the crust, in a medium bowl, stir together the graham crackers, butter, brown sugar, salt, and cinnamon until combined and the crumbs are thoroughly moistened. Transfer the mixture into the prepared pan, and evenly and firmly press it into the bottom and halfway up the sides—you can use your fingers for this or, as I prefer, a glass with a flat bottom. Freeze the crust for 20 minutes, then bake until lightly toasted, about 8 minutes. Transfer the pan to a wire rack and allow the crust to cool completely before filling. ⟶

NOTE: Dulce de leche can be found at the grocery store with the cans of sweetened condensed milk (my preferred brand is La Lechera) or in a jar with the jams; using store-bought makes this cake a breeze. In a pinch, though, you can make it at home. Remove the label from a can of sweetened condensed milk and place the can in a medium saucepan and cover with at least 2 inches of water. Bring the water to a boil, then reduce the heat, cover (leaving the lid slightly ajar), and simmer for 3 hours. Add more water as needed to keep the can fully submerged. Allow it to cool completely before using.

◆ To make the filling, in the bowl of a stand mixer fitted with the whisk attachment, whip the heavy cream on medium-high speed until medium-firm peaks form. Scrape it into a medium bowl and refrigerate.

◆ In the same mixer bowl (no need to wash!), now fitted with the paddle attachment, sift in the powdered sugar and add the cream cheese. Beat on medium speed until light and fluffy, 3 to 4 minutes. Scrape down the bottom and sides of the bowl and add the dulce de leche, vanilla, and salt. Beat on medium speed until the filling is light, fluffy, and no lumps remain, another 2 to 3 minutes.

◆ Using a silicone spatula, gently fold one-third of the chilled whipped cream into the filling until just incorporated. Fold in the rest of the whipped cream in two batches. Scrape the filling into the cooled crust. Use a spoon or a small offset spatula to evenly spread and smooth out the top. Chill in the refrigerator overnight and for up to 3 days.

◆ Once the cake is completely set, make the topping. In a small saucepan over very low heat, stir the dulce de leche and heavy cream until smooth. You want it to be just barely warm—if it's too hot, it will melt the filling. Let it cool a bit if necessary. Using a spoon or small offset spatula, spread the topping evenly over the filling, leaving a small space between topping and crust so the cheesecake peeks out. Return the cheesecake to the refrigerator until ready to serve.

◆ Use a paring knife or offset spatula to loosen the crust from the sides of the pan before unmolding. Just before serving, lightly sprinkle the topping all over with flaky sea salt. Use a sharp (not serrated) knife to cut slices.

◆ This cake keeps well wrapped in the refrigerator for 4 to 5 days. It also freezes nicely for up to 2 months—no need to thaw: it's delicious straight from the freezer.

OLIVE OIL CAKE

2 tablespoons finely grated
  citrus zest
1¼ cups (250 g) granulated
  sugar
2 cups *minus* 1½ tablespoons
  (250 g) all-purpose flour
1 teaspoon kosher salt
½ teaspoon baking powder
½ teaspoon baking soda
3 eggs, at room temperature
1 cup (235 ml) mild and
  buttery or fruity olive oil,
  plus more for serving
¾ cup (180 ml) buttermilk or
  plain whole-milk yogurt, at
  room temperature
¼ cup (60 ml) freshly
  squeezed citrus juice
Crème fraîche and seasonal
  fruit jam or compote (see
  page 139), for serving

On the day this cake is baked, it has a wonderful golden crisped exterior, but as it ages, the flavors deepen and the crumb softens. The profile of the olive oil you use will be accentuated here, so be sure to taste it first. Stay away from varieties that are grassy and robust; instead, opt for one that is bold and fruit-forward or, if you're looking for a less assertive taste, mild and buttery. You can use whatever citrus you have on hand.

MAKES 6 TO 8 SERVINGS

◆ Preheat the oven to 350 degrees F. Grease a 9-inch springform or a deep 9-inch cake pan and line the bottom with parchment paper.

◆ In a medium bowl, use your fingers to rub the zest into the sugar until it has taken on the citrus color and perfume. Whisk in the flour, salt, baking powder, and baking soda. In a large bowl, whisk together the eggs, oil, buttermilk, and citrus juice until smooth. Add the flour mixture and whisk until just combined.

◆ Scrape the batter into the prepared pan. Bake until the cake is golden brown and firm and a tester inserted into the center comes out clean, 50 to 60 minutes. Transfer the pan to a wire rack and allow the cake to cool for 20 minutes before unmolding. Invert onto a plate, remove the parchment, then invert onto a wire rack. Allow the cake to cool completely.

◆ Serve with a dollop of crème fraîche and jam on the side, and finish with a drizzle of olive oil. This cake keeps well wrapped at room temperature for 4 to 5 days.

RHUBARB-CARDAMOM UPSIDE-DOWN CAKE

For the topping
¼ cup (55 g) unsalted butter
¾ cup (150 g) packed light brown sugar
Pinch of kosher salt
12 to 16 ounces (340 to 445 g) rhubarb, trimmed and kept whole or cut into 2-inch-thick pieces (3 to 4 cups)

For the cake
1⅓ cups plus 2 tablespoons (185 g) all-purpose flour
1½ teaspoons finely crushed cardamom seeds, or 1 teaspoon ground cardamom
1¼ teaspoons baking powder
1 teaspoon kosher salt
⅛ teaspoon baking soda
½ cup (115 g) unsalted butter, at room temperature
¾ cup (150 g) granulated sugar
¼ cup (50 g) packed light brown sugar
2 eggs, at room temperature
1½ teaspoons vanilla extract
½ cup (120 g) plain whole-milk yogurt, at room temperature

Cardamom's fragrant, almost musky flavor lends itself particularly well to baked goods where fruit—or in this case, vegetable—is the star. The tartness of rhubarb plays with the sweetness of the caramel topping and the spice itself. In other seasons, try stone fruit, apples, pears, or cranberries.

Play around with the design of your rhubarb topping: you can trim whole stalks to fit the pan and line them up side by side; slice stalks into pieces and arrange them in concentric circles; or, if you cut slices on the diagonal, nestle them together like a puzzle to create different patterns.

MAKES 6 TO 8 SERVINGS

• Preheat the oven to 350 degrees F. Grease the sides of a 10-inch cast-iron skillet or a deep 9-inch cake pan.

• To make the topping, set the prepared pan over medium-low heat. Add the butter and melt, then whisk in the brown sugar and salt to combine. At first, the mixture won't emulsify, but after 2 to 3 minutes, it will thicken into a smooth paste and begin to simmer. Remove the pan from the heat and arrange the rhubarb, flat side down, in the bottom in an even layer. Set aside.

• To make the cake, in a small bowl, whisk together the flour, cardamom, baking powder, salt, and baking soda.

• In the bowl of a stand mixer fitted with the paddle attachment, beat the butter and both sugars on medium speed until light and fluffy, 4 to 5 minutes, scraping down the bottom and sides of the bowl as needed. Add the eggs one at a time, beating to fully incorporate after each addition. Add the vanilla and mix to combine.

• Reduce the speed to low and add the flour mixture to the batter in three additions, alternating with two additions of the yogurt, mixing until just combined and scraping down the bowl as needed. Scrape the batter over the rhubarb in the pan and smooth out the top.

• Bake until the cake is lightly golden and a tester inserted into the center of the cake (but not the topping) comes out clean, 35 to 45 minutes if baking in a cake pan and 40 to 50 minutes if baking in a skillet. Transfer the pan to a wire rack and allow the cake to cool for 20 minutes. Invert a serving platter or cake plate over the pan and, using oven mitts for protection, flip the whole thing over. The cake should slip right out of the pan, but if not, knock the plate against the counter a few times to loosen the cake. Any rhubarb that sticks to the pan can be removed with an offset spatula and returned to the cake.

• This cake is best served warm on the day it is baked, but it keeps well wrapped at room temperature for 2 to 3 days.

APPLE SHARLOTKA

1 cup (130 g) all-purpose flour
½ teaspoon baking powder
½ teaspoon kosher salt
3 to 4 medium apples (about
  2 pounds, or 8 cups),
  peeled, cored, and cut into
  ¼-inch slices
2 tablespoons freshly
  squeezed lemon juice
1 to 1½ teaspoons finely
  grated lemon zest
4 eggs, at room temperature
1 cup (200 g) granulated sugar
1 teaspoon vanilla extract
⅓ cup (50 g) golden raisins
1 tablespoon turbinado sugar
  (optional)
Powdered sugar, for dusting
Whipped cream or Greek
  yogurt, for serving

I'm usually inspired to make this classic Russian tea cake last minute when the desire to bake hits and I happen to have a bowl of apples on hand. It comes together quickly, and once in the oven, the fruit softens and the batter transforms into a wonderful melt-in-your-mouth sponge. The top also develops a thin crust that shatters when you cut into it—my favorite part! I'll have it for dessert only to find myself eating it for breakfast *and* as an afternoon snack the next day. Look for apples that are sweet-tart and firm, such as Jonagold, Honeycrisp, or Pink Lady.

MAKES 6 TO 8 SERVINGS

• Preheat the oven to 350 degrees F. Grease a 9-inch spring-form pan and line the bottom with parchment paper.

• In a small bowl, whisk together the flour, baking powder, and salt. In a medium bowl, toss the apples with the lemon juice and zest.

• In the bowl of a stand mixer fitted with the whisk attachment, beat the eggs and sugar on high speed until thick ribbons form (see page 42), 8 to 10 minutes. Add the vanilla and mix to combine.

• Sift half of the flour mixture into the batter and, using the whisk or a silicone spatula, gently fold it in by hand until just combined. Sift and fold in the remaining flour mixture.

• Arrange half of the apples in an even layer in the bottom of the pan and top with the golden raisins. Pour the batter over them and smooth out the top. Slightly tuck the remaining apple slices on their flat sides into the batter (I like to create a swirl by working from the outer edge toward the center, slightly overlapping each slice). Sprinkle all over with the turbinado sugar.

◆ Bake until the cake is a deep golden brown and firm and a tester inserted into the center comes out clean, 55 to 70 minutes. Transfer the pan to a wire rack and allow the cake to cool for 30 minutes before unmolding. Dust with powdered sugar and serve warm or cooled with whipped cream or Greek yogurt. This cake keeps well wrapped at room temperature for 4 to 5 days.

WHOLE-CITRUS ALMOND CAKE

2 small organic Meyer lemons,
well scrubbed
1 small organic orange, such
as Cara Cara, Valencia,
or heirloom navel, well
scrubbed
6 eggs, at room temperature
1 cup plus 2½ tablespoons
(225 g) granulated sugar
Finely grated zest of 1 lemon
1½ teaspoons vanilla extract
1 teaspoon kosher salt
2¼ cups (225 g) almond flour
2 teaspoons baking powder

For the glaze
½ cup (60 g) powdered sugar
1½ to 2 tablespoons freshly
squeezed Meyer or regular
lemon juice, strained

The first time I had this cake it was revelatory. The recipe's roots are Sephardic, and it became more widely known through the work of great cookbook author Claudia Roden. Boil whole citrus, blitz the softened fruit into a puree, and then whisk it together with eggs, sugar, and almond flour—that's it. The bittersweet result is essentially citrus marmalade in cake form, with a texture that's soft and lush. To finish, drizzle with a citrus glaze as I do here, top with a soft chocolate ganache (see variation), or leave it plain.

I love the sweet perfume of Meyer lemons here—tempered a bit with orange—but try it with whatever citrus you have on hand; start with a little less than a pound of citrus (anywhere from 375 to 425 grams).

MAKES 6 TO 8 SERVINGS

✦ Place the whole lemons and orange in a medium pot, cover with water, and bring to a boil over high heat. Reduce the heat to low, cover, and gently simmer for 1½ to 2 hours, or until the citrus is very soft and tender (I find the lemons usually cook faster than the orange). Add more water as needed to keep the fruit submerged; it's OK if they split. Remove the citrus with a slotted spoon and allow to cool completely before breaking them open with your fingers to remove the seeds and any hard bits.

✦ In a food processor, puree the citrus, peel and all. You should have 1¼ to 1½ cups (325 to 365 g) of puree, depending on the size of the fruit. The puree can be made in advance and stored in an airtight container in the refrigerator for 3 to 4 days or in the freezer for up to 2 months.

✦ Preheat the oven to 375 degrees F. Grease a 9-inch spring-form pan or a deep 9-inch cake pan and line the bottom with parchment paper.

✦ In a large bowl, first whisk the eggs, then whisk in the granulated sugar, lemon zest, vanilla, salt, and all of the citrus puree. Add the almond flour and baking powder and whisk until just combined—there will be some lumps, but that's OK; you don't want to overmix.

✦ Scrape the batter into the prepared pan and smooth out the top. Bake until the cake begins to brown and a tester inserted into the center comes out clean, 40 to 50 minutes. Remove the cake from the oven and let it cool for 20 minutes before unmolding. Invert onto a plate, remove the parchment, then invert onto a wire rack. Allow the cake to cool completely.

✦ To make the glaze, in a medium bowl, stir together the powdered sugar and 1½ tablespoons lemon juice until smooth. Add a bit more lemon juice if needed to achieve a thin, runny consistency.

✦ Drizzle the glaze over the top of the cooled cake and serve. This cake keeps well wrapped at room temperature for 2 to 3 days, at which point you can refrigerate it for another day or two.

VARIATION: For a chocolate ganache topping, see page 33—use a half portion for this cake. Slowly pour the ganache over the cooled cake, starting in the center and gradually making your way to the edges. You can either let it run down the sides or leave it as a smooth, even layer on top. Let the ganache set for at least 1 hour before serving.

APRICOT CORNMEAL SKILLET CAKE

1¼ cups (165 g) all-purpose flour

⅔ cup (135 g) granulated sugar

½ to ⅔ cup (80 g to 105 g) finely ground cornmeal (see Note)

2 teaspoons baking powder

1¼ teaspoons kosher salt

½ cup (115 g) unsalted butter, plus more for greasing

¼ cup (85 g) honey

¾ cup (180 g) plain whole-milk yogurt, at room temperature

2 eggs, at room temperature

1½ teaspoons vanilla extract

6 to 7 ripe (but not mushy) medium apricots, halved and pitted

3 tablespoons turbinado sugar

Vanilla ice cream, whipped cream, or heavy cream, for serving

NOTE: For a more pronounced corn flavor, use the greater amount—the cake texture will just be a little bit denser.

Cornmeal cakes, with their rustic texture and sunshine hue, beg to be paired with juicy, sweet fruit. In this case, tangy, ripe apricots are nestled right into the batter, and a bit of honey adds floral notes that play off the fruit. Best of all, this cake is baked and served in a cast-iron pan, which makes it a quick and easy weeknight treat. Experiment with other fruit, such as berries, stone fruit, or figs.

MAKES 8 TO 10 SERVINGS

◆ Preheat the oven to 350 degrees F. In a large bowl, whisk together the flour, granulated sugar, cornmeal, baking powder, and salt.

◆ Set a 10-inch well-seasoned cast-iron skillet over low heat and add the butter and honey. Warm just until the butter has melted and the honey, if it was crystallized, has liquified. Remove the pan from the heat. Make a well in the center of the dry ingredients and scrape the butter mixture into the bowl. Add the yogurt, eggs, and vanilla, and whisk until combined.

◆ Grease the sides of the pan with butter before scraping the batter into the pan; spread it evenly, and smooth out the top. Top the batter with the apricot halves, cut side up, and sprinkle all over with the turbinado sugar. Bake the cake until a tester inserted into the center comes out with a few moist crumbs attached, 45 to 55 minutes (it will continue baking after you remove it from the oven). Serve warm with vanilla ice cream, slightly sweetened whipped cream, or a drizzle of heavy cream. This cake is best served warm on the day it is baked, but it will keep well wrapped at room temperature for to 2 to 3 days.

TURKISH COFFEE CRUMB CAKE

For the crumb
1 cup (130 g) all-purpose flour
3 tablespoons (20 g) rye flour
   or all-purpose flour
¼ cup (50 g) packed light
   brown sugar
1¼ teaspoons instant
   espresso powder
½ teaspoon kosher salt
¼ teaspoon finely crushed
   cardamom seeds, or a
   generous pinch of ground
   cardamom
¼ teaspoon ground cinnamon
¼ teaspoon ground coriander
7 tablespoons (100 g) unsalted
   butter, melted

For the cake
1¼ cups (165 g) all-purpose
   flour
3 tablespoons (20 g) rye flour
   or all-purpose flour
1½ tablespoons instant
   espresso powder
1½ teaspoons baking powder
1 teaspoon kosher salt
1 teaspoon finely crushed
   cardamom seeds, or
   ¾ teaspoon ground
   cardamom
½ teaspoon ground cinnamon
½ teaspoon ground coriander
¼ teaspoon baking soda
1 cup (200 g) packed light
   brown sugar

CONTINUED

What sets Turkish coffee apart from regular drip is the fact that it's brewed with grounds and sugar boiled directly in water. The result is rich, intense, and—because it's served in a beautiful filigreed demitasse cup—simply unforgettable. This cake, shot through with espresso and spices like cardamom and coriander, plays off of the moody feeling Turkish coffee inspires. Slightly milky rye flour and a delightful crumb topping lighten things up a bit. Not surprisingly, it pairs especially well with a cup of hot coffee, whatever the variety.

MAKES 6 TO 8 SERVINGS

◆ Preheat the oven to 350 degrees F. Grease a 9-inch spring-form pan and line with parchment paper.

◆ To make the crumb, in a medium bowl, stir together both flours, sugar, espresso powder, salt, cardamom, cinnamon, and coriander. Add the melted butter, and stir until combined and uneven crumbs form. Set aside.

◆ To make the cake, in a small bowl, whisk together both flours, espresso powder, baking powder, salt, cardamom, cinnamon, coriander, and baking soda.

◆ In the bowl of a stand mixer fitted with the paddle attachment, beat the sugar and butter on medium speed until light and fluffy, 4 to 5 minutes, scraping down the bottom and sides of the bowl often. Add the eggs one at a time, beating to fully incorporate after each addition and scraping down the bowl as needed. Add the vanilla and mix to combine. ⟶

¾ cup (170 g) unsalted butter, at room temperature
2 eggs, at room temperature
1½ teaspoons vanilla extract
¾ cup (180 g) sour cream, at room temperature
¾ cup (85 g) toasted walnuts, chopped (optional)

♦ Reduce the speed to low and add the flour mixture to the batter in three additions, alternating with two additions of the sour cream, mixing until just combined and scraping down the bowl as needed. Stir in the walnuts.

♦ Scrape the batter into the prepared pan and smooth out the top. Sprinkle the top evenly with the crumb topping. Bake the cake until a tester inserted into the center comes out clean, 40 to 45 minutes. Allow the cake to cool completely in the pan before removing and serving. This cake keeps well wrapped at room temperature for 2 to 3 days.

VARIATION: Turkish coffee is oftentimes served with a square of chocolate or Turkish delight—stir in ¼ cup (40 g) finely chopped semisweet or bittersweet chocolate along with the walnuts to mimic this pairing.

TOASTING NUTS

Toasting nuts enhances their flavor and gives them a pleasant crunch. To toast, preheat the oven or toaster oven to 350 degrees F. Spread nuts in an even layer on a rimmed baked sheet, set a timer (most important!) for 8 to 12 minutes, and bake, stirring occasionally to ensure even cooking. Pine nuts, pistachios, and thinly sliced or slivered almonds will take closer to 5 to 8 minutes. The nuts will be a shade darker, smell toasted, and will snap when you bite into one. Cool completely before using.

FLOURLESS CHOCOLATE CRUNCH CAKE WITH PORT CHERRIES

8 ounces (225 g) bittersweet chocolate, finely chopped

¾ cup (170 g) unsalted butter, cubed

3 tablespoons (20 g) cocoa nibs, finely chopped (optional)

6 egg yolks, at room temperature

½ cup (100 g) packed light brown sugar

1 tablespoon brandy or dark rum (optional)

1 teaspoon kosher salt

4 egg whites, at room temperature

¼ cup plus 2 tablespoons (70 g) granulated sugar

Powdered sugar or cocoa powder, for dusting

Whipped cream, for serving

Port Cherries (see page 76) or fresh cherries or berries, for serving

One of my favorite dessert cookbooks is Gina DePalma's *Dolce Italiano.* This chocolate cake is a riff on her Chocolate and Walnut Torte. Her nontraditional use of brown sugar underscores the flavor of chocolate, and the generous number of egg yolks keep the cake fudgy. I've added cocoa nibs for crunch and cherries—suspended in an inky port wine syrup—as a boozy finishing touch. Serve it when you want your meal to end on a simple and elegant note, or when nothing less than intensely chocolatey will do.

MAKES 6 TO 8 SERVINGS

⟡ Preheat the oven to 350 degrees F. Line the bottom of a 9-inch springform pan with parchment paper.

⟡ Fill a medium pot with an inch of water and bring to a gentle simmer over medium heat. In a large heatproof bowl, combine the chocolate, butter, and cocoa nibs and set over the pot (make sure the bottom of the bowl doesn't touch the water). Stir occasionally to encourage melting and prevent the chocolate from burning. Once the mixture has melted and becomes smooth and glossy, remove the bowl from the pot, wipe the underside, and set it aside to cool to lukewarm.

⟡ In a medium bowl, whisk together the egg yolks, brown sugar, brandy, and salt to combine. Slowly stir the egg yolk mixture into the melted chocolate until fully combined. Set aside. $\longrightarrow$

◆ In the bowl of a stand mixer fitted with the whisk attachment, whip the egg whites on medium speed until thick and dense but still runny, about 2 minutes. With the mixer running, gradually add the granulated sugar 1 or 2 tablespoons at a time. Continue to beat until soft peaks form (see page 51), 1 to 2 minutes.

◆ With the silicone spatula, gently fold the meringue into the chocolate mixture until just combined and no obvious white streaks remain—do not overfold! Carefully scrape the batter into the prepared pan and smooth out the top.

◆ Bake the cake for 30 to 35 minutes. The edges will rise up first, but eventually the center will puff and the top will begin to crack. Transfer the pan to a wire rack and allow the cake to cool—it will start to fall as it does—for 15 minutes before running a knife around the edges of the pan and unmolding. Allow the cake to cool completely. If desired, invert the cake onto a plate, remove the parchment, and invert it again onto a serving platter.

◆ Dust the cake with powdered sugar and serve with a dollop of whipped cream and a generous spoonful of port cherries and their syrup. This cake keeps well wrapped at room temperature for up to 3 days.

Port Cherries

2 cups (310 g) fresh or frozen
   pitted cherries
1/3 cup (80 ml) plus
   2 teaspoons ruby or tawny
   port, divided
1/4 cup (50 g) granulated sugar
1/4 teaspoon kosher salt
1½ teaspoons cornstarch

A quick simmer turns cherries into glistening sweet orbs, their flavor concentrated and infused with port and vice versa. As for the port, no need to shell out on a fancy bottle; the cheap stuff will work just fine.

MAKES A SCANT 2 CUPS

✦ Combine the cherries, 1/3 cup (80 ml) of the port, sugar, and salt in a medium saucepan. Bring to a boil, then reduce the heat and simmer, stirring often, until the cherries have released their juices and begin to collapse, 10 to 12 minutes. In a small bowl, combine the cornstarch with the remaining 2 teaspoons port and stir into the compote when it's nearly ready. Allow the compote to return to a full simmer and cook for another 30 seconds before removing from the heat. Let cool before using. The cherries keep well stored in an airtight container in the refrigerator for up to 1 week.

STRAWBERRIES-AND-CREAM CAKE

1 cup (225 g) unsalted butter
5 eggs, at room temperature
  (see Note)
1 cup (200 g) granulated sugar
1½ cups (195 g) all-purpose
  flour, plus more for dusting
1½ teaspoons baking powder
1 teaspoon kosher salt
2 teaspoons finely grated
  lemon zest
1½ teaspoons vanilla extract
Powdered sugar, for dusting

**For the macerated
  strawberries**
1¼ pounds (565 g) fresh
  strawberries, hulled, halved
  or quartered, depending
  on size
3 to 5 tablespoons granulated
  sugar, depending on
  sweetness of fruit
1 tablespoon freshly
  squeezed lemon juice
1½ teaspoons vanilla extract
  or vanilla bean paste
Pinch of kosher salt

For the whipped cream
1 cup (235 ml) cold heavy
  cream
¾ cup (165 g) sour cream or
  crème fraîche
2 tablespoons granulated
  sugar

This pound-meets-sponge cake (adapted from Claudia Fleming's *The Last Course*) was inspired by the store-bought little sponge cake shells that, as a kid, I would hide under a pile of fruit and Cool Whip. This grown-up version is filled with macerated strawberries—their juices brightly and deliciously soaking through the sponge—and a puff of whipped cream laced with said juices and tangy sour cream. The cake is delightfully light, so you won't think twice about reaching for a second slice. To streamline preparation, make the cake and strawberries the day before. That way all you have to do is whip the cream before assembling.

MAKES 8 TO 10 SERVINGS

◆ Preheat the oven to 350 degrees F. Lightly grease a deep 9-inch cake pan. Line the bottom with parchment paper and dust the inside lightly with flour.

◆ In a small saucepan, melt the butter on medium-low heat and set aside to cool.

◆ In the bowl of a stand mixer fitted with the whisk attachment, beat the eggs and granulated sugar on high speed until thick ribbons form (see page 42), 6 to 8 minutes. In a medium bowl, sift together the flour, baking powder, and salt. Using a silicone spatula, gently but confidently fold the lemon zest and one-third of the flour mixture into the egg mixture by hand until combined. Fold in the rest of the flour mixture in two batches. $\longrightarrow$

◆ In the empty bowl that held the flour, whisk together 1 cup (about 100 g) of the batter with the slightly warm melted butter and vanilla to thoroughly combine. Pour this mixture back into the batter and gently fold to incorporate—there shouldn't be any streaks. Gently scrape the batter into the prepared pan and smooth out the top.

◆ Bake until the cake springs back when pressed and a tester inserted in the center comes out clean, 30 to 35 minutes. Transfer the pan to a wire rack and allow the cake to cool completely before assembling.

◆ To make the macerated strawberries, in a large bowl, toss the strawberries with the sugar, lemon juice, vanilla, and salt. Let sit for 45 to 60 minutes, stirring occasionally. The strawberries will soften significantly and release their juices to create a pool of bright-red syrup. Use a fork or the back of a spoon to crush the strawberries to create a jammy mash. Set aside. If making ahead of time, cover and refrigerate for up to 1 day.

◆ Just before assembling, make the tangy whipped cream. First measure out ¼ cup (70 ml) of syrup from the macerated strawberries—it's OK if some fruit pieces are in there. In the bowl of a stand mixer fitted with the whisk attachment, whip the cream on medium speed until soft peaks form. Pause, add the strawberry syrup, sour cream, and sugar, and mix on medium speed to incorporate. Continue to mix until the cream has thickened and firm peaks form. It will taste like strawberries and cream distilled into one bite.

◆ To assemble the cake (see page 83), first cut it in half crosswise with a serrated knife using a gentle sawing motion. Transfer the bottom layer (cut side up) to a serving platter or cake plate. Top the cake with the macerated strawberries and then drizzle with a few spoonfuls of the syrup—just enough to evenly soak the strawberries and cake layer.

◆ Dollop the whipped cream over the berries and use an off-set spatula to evenly smooth the top. Top with the other cake layer (cut side down). Let the cake chill in the refrigerator for 30 minutes to set the whipped cream. Then let it sit at room temperature for 30 minutes before dusting with powdered sugar and serving with any remaining strawberry syrup on the side for drizzling. This cake is best the day it is made but will keep in the refrigerator well wrapped for 2 to 3 days.

VARIATION: For an easier alternative that ventures into British territory, substitute jam for the fresh berries.

PREPPING CAKE LAYERS

- Make sure the cakes are completely cool before assembly or storage. If baking the cakes ahead of time, wrap them tightly with plastic wrap. If assembling within a day or two, leave them at room temperature. Otherwise freeze the cakes for up to 2 months—assemble and frost them while frozen and allow them extra time to come to room temperature before serving.

- If your cake has a domed center, you can even it out. Place one hand on top of the cake to steady it, then use a long serrated knife to cut crosswise through the cake in a gentle sawing motion (a turntable is useful here, as you can rotate the cake while you cut) just below the dome. Only cut off what is needed to even out the top. Discard the dome piece or set it aside to snack on or make cake pops with.

- If you have time, place the cooled cake in the freezer for 15 to 20 minutes—this will make it much easier to work with.

- To cut a cake in half or in thirds, first place it on an even surface or turntable. Use a long serrated knife to score a line around the outside of the cake where you plan to cut it (if it's helpful, you can use a ruler here). Then, placing one hand on top of the cake to steady it, slowly cut through the cake in a gentle sawing motion, frequently checking to make sure it's level, and rotating the cake as you go. Carefully lift off the top layer and set it aside. At this point, either move the bottom layer to a serving platter or keep it on the turntable. Proceed to frost.

COCONUT-LIME CREAM CAKE WITH FLUFFY MARSHMALLOW FROSTING

2½ cups *minus* 1 tablespoon (320 g) all-purpose flour
1 tablespoon baking powder
1¼ teaspoons kosher salt
1½ tablespoons finely grated lime zest (from about 2 large limes), plus more for topping
1½ cups (300 g) granulated sugar
¾ cup (170 g) unsalted butter, at room temperature
½ cup (160 g) sweetened cream of coconut (see Note)
4 eggs, separated, at room temperature
1½ teaspoons vanilla extract
1 cup (235 ml) buttermilk, at room temperature
2 cups (170 g) sweetened shredded coconut, plus more for topping

For the frosting
1⅓ cups (265 g) granulated sugar
⅔ cup (170 g) egg whites (from about 5 eggs)
5 teaspoons freshly squeezed lime juice
½ teaspoon cream of tartar
½ teaspoon kosher salt
1 teaspoon vanilla extract

Put the lime in the coconut and bake it all up! This classic layer cake is soft, tender, and perfumed with the flavors of coconut and lime. A fluffy marshmallow frosting provides a lovely counterpoint to the rich-tasting cake and adds pretty swoops and swirls to boot. While whipping the egg whites separately is a bit of a pain, it is what gives the cake its light, melt-in-your-mouth texture. For best results, make the frosting in a stand mixer.

MAKES 8 TO 10 SERVINGS

◆ Preheat the oven to 350 degrees F. Lightly grease two 9-inch cake pans and line the bottoms with parchment paper.

◆ In a medium bowl, whisk together the flour, baking powder, and salt.

◆ In the bowl of a stand mixer fitted with the paddle attachment, use your fingers to rub the zest into the sugar until it has taken on the citrus color and perfume. Add the butter and beat on medium speed until light and fluffy, 4 to 5 minutes, scraping down the bottom and sides of the bowl often. Add the cream of coconut and beat for another minute to fully incorporate. Add the egg yolks one at a time, beating to fully incorporate after each addition and scraping down the bowl as needed. Add the vanilla and mix to combine.

◆ Reduce the speed to low and add the flour mixture in three additions, alternating with three additions of buttermilk, mixing until just combined and scraping down the bowl as needed. Stir in the shredded coconut.

• If you have a hand mixer, in a separate clean medium bowl using clean beaters, beat the egg whites on medium speed until firm peaks form (see page 51). If using the stand mixer again, transfer the batter to a separate large bowl, and thoroughly wash and dry the dirty bowl before beating the egg whites with a whisk attachment. Gently fold one-third of the egg whites into the batter until just combined to lighten it (it will be hard at first because the batter is so thick), then repeat with the remaining egg whites.

• Divide the batter evenly between the prepared pans and gently smooth out the tops. Bake, rotating and switching their positions halfway through, until the cakes feel firm on top and a tester inserted into the centers comes out clean, 25 to 30 minutes. Transfer the pans to a wire rack and allow the cakes to cool completely. (The frosting sets rather quickly, so they must be fully cooled and leveled, if needed, before proceeding.)

• To make the marshmallow frosting, first fill a medium pot with 1 inch of water and bring to a gentle simmer over medium heat. If you have a stand mixer with a bowl-lift design, you can use its mixing bowl to cook the egg-white mixture. Otherwise, in a medium heatproof bowl, whisk together the sugar, egg whites, lime juice, cream of tartar, and salt. Set the bowl over the pot (make sure the bottom doesn't touch the water). Cook, stirring and scraping the bowl constantly with a silicone spatula, until the temperature of the mixture has reached 175 degrees F on a digital or candy thermometer. The sugar should have dissolved, and the liquid should feel smooth when rubbed between your fingers. $\longrightarrow$

* Scrape the mixture into the bowl of a stand mixer fitted with the whisk attachment. Whip on medium-high speed until the meringue is glossy, holds stiff peaks (see page 51), and starts to ball up inside the whisk, about 5 minutes. Add the vanilla and mix to combine. Use the frosting immediately.

* To assemble the cake (see pages 94–95), place one of the layers (top side up) on a cake stand or plate. Tuck strips of parchment paper under the edge of the cake to keep the plate clean. Use an offset spatula to generously cover the layer with about 1½ cups of the frosting. Center the second cake layer (top side down) over the frosted layer and nestle it on top. Spread the remaining frosting over the top and sides, making swoops and swirls with the spatula or a spoon. If desired, cover the entire cake with shredded or flaked coconut, gently pressing it into the frosting with your fingers. Sprinkle lime zest over the top.

* Serve the cake immediately or cover it loosely and refrigerate for up to 1 day—allow it to come to room temperature before serving.

CARROT CAKE WITH BROWNED BUTTER– CREAM CHEESE FROSTING

2⅔ cups (345 g) all-purpose flour, plus more for dusting
1 cup plus 2 tablespoons (225 g) firmly packed light brown sugar
1 cup (200 g) granulated sugar
2 teaspoons kosher salt
1½ teaspoons baking powder
1½ teaspoons ground cinnamon
1 teaspoon ground ginger
1 teaspoon baking soda
½ teaspoon lightly packed freshly grated nutmeg
½ teaspoon ground cardamom, cloves, or allspice
4 eggs, at room temperature
1⅓ cups (315 ml) neutral oil, such as canola or safflower
½ cup (120 ml) buttermilk or plain whole-milk yogurt, at room temperature
1 tablespoon vanilla extract
1 pound (445 g) coarsely grated carrots (about 3 cups)
1⅓ cups (150 g) toasted walnuts or pecans, chopped, plus more for garnish
1 cup (150 g) golden raisins, tart cherries, chopped dates, or apricots (optional)
Flaked coconut, for garnish

I've never come across a more beloved yet divisive cake. Some folks are purists, eschewing any add-ins. Others are open to inclusions, such as nuts, dried fruit, and coconut, but are particular about which ones. I myself am partial to toasted nuts and golden raisins, but feel free to omit or swap out either ingredient for an equal amount of shredded coconut. As for the icing on the cake, I think we can all agree that it's not carrot cake without cream cheese frosting. I've taken some liberty and added nutty browned butter. I hope you don't mind.

MAKES 8 TO 10 SERVINGS

⁕ Preheat the oven to 350 degrees F. Grease two deep 8- or 9-inch round cake pans and dust the insides lightly with flour.

⁕ In a large bowl, whisk together the flour, both sugars, salt, baking powder, cinnamon, ginger, baking soda, nutmeg, and cardamom. Add the eggs, oil, buttermilk, and vanilla and whisk until just combined and smooth. Use a silicone spatula to fold in carrots, walnuts, and raisins.

⁕ Divide the batter evenly between the prepared pans and bake, rotating and switching their positions halfway through, until a tester inserted into the centers comes out clean, 40 to 50 minutes for 8-inch pans or 35 to 45 minutes for 9-inch pans. Transfer the pans to a wire rack and allow the cakes to cool completely before assembling.

For the frosting

1 cup (225 g) unsalted butter
16 ounces (445 g) full-fat
cream cheese, at room
temperature
2 tablespoons heavy cream
or milk
1½ teaspoons vanilla extract
½ teaspoon apple cider
vinegar
¼ teaspoon kosher salt
2 cups (240 g) powdered
sugar

NOTE: To make a regular
cream cheese frosting, simply don't brown the butter;
proceed with the recipe as
written using room-
temperature butter and
replace the vinegar with
1 teaspoon lemon juice.

* To make the frosting, first melt the butter in a small saucepan with a light-colored bottom (this will make it easier to check browning) over medium heat. The butter will foam and start to vigorously bubble. Continue cooking at a low simmer, swirl-ing the pan occasionally, until the bubbling subsides and the butter begins to brown and smell nutty. Remove from the heat and allow the butter to keep browning in the pan—the aim is a golden caramel color. Transfer the butter to a shallow bowl and refrigerate until solid.

* In the bowl of a stand mixer fitted with the paddle attach-ment, beat the solidified butter on medium speed until light and fluffy, about 2 minutes. Scrape down the bottom and sides of the bowl, then add the cream cheese, heavy cream, vanilla, vinegar, and salt. Sift in the powdered sugar. Gradually increas-ing the speed to medium, beat for about 1 minute or until combined. Season with more salt to taste. The frosting can be used immediately or refrigerated for up to 2 weeks—allow it to sit at room temperature for 20 minutes before using.

* To assemble the cake (see pages 94–95), place one of the lay-ers (top side up) on a cake stand or plate. Tuck strips of parch-ment paper under the edge of the cake to keep the plate clean. Top the layer with about 1 cup of the frosting and use an offset spatula to spread it into an even layer. Center the second cake layer (top side down) over the frosted layer and nestle it on top. Using as little frosting as possible, spread a very thin crumb coat over the top and sides of the cake and fill any gaps. If possible, refrigerate the cake for 20 minutes to set it.

* Spread the remaining frosting evenly all over the top and sides of the cake. If desired, garnish with nuts or shredded or flaked coconut, depending on the filling. Serve the cake the same day or refrigerate for 2 to 3 days—allow it to come to room temperature before serving.

YELLOW BIRTHDAY CAKE WITH WHIPPED MALT CHOCOLATE BUTTERCREAM

3 cups (390 g) all-purpose flour
¼ cup (30 g) malted milk powder
1 tablespoon baking powder
1 teaspoon kosher salt
3 eggs, at room temperature
3 egg yolks, at room temperature
2 tablespoons neutral oil, such as canola or safflower
2½ teaspoons vanilla extract
2 cups (400 g) granulated sugar
1 cup (225 g) unsalted butter, at room temperature
1 cup (235 ml) whole milk, at room temperature

For the frosting
½ cup (65 g) malted milk powder
¼ cup (50 g) packed light brown sugar
6½ ounces (185 g) bittersweet chocolate, finely chopped
1 cup (235 ml) heavy cream
1 cup (225 g) unsalted butter, at room temperature
1¾ cups (210 g) powdered sugar
1½ teaspoons vanilla extract
½ teaspoon kosher salt

When I was kid, I was always asked "Chocolate or vanilla?" when it came to dessert. I believe that the two are best not kept apart but matched together. This classic yellow cake is filled and decorated with a whipped chocolate ganache frosting. It's rich yet light, silky, and good enough to be eaten by the spoonful. But to really make the components sing, I've turned to another ingredient of my childhood: malted milk powder. The powdered grain extract brings a toasted, butterscotch-y depth of flavor that amplifies both the vanilla in the cake and the chocolate in the frosting. Find it either in the baking aisle next to the sweetened condensed milk or with the powdered hot cocoa.

MAKES 8 TO 10 SERVINGS

◆ Preheat the oven to 350 degrees F. Grease two 9-inch cake pans and line the bottoms with parchment paper.

◆ In a medium bowl, whisk together the flour, malted milk powder, baking powder, and salt. In a small bowl, whisk together the eggs, egg yolks, oil, and vanilla to combine.

◆ In the bowl of a stand mixer fitted with the paddle attachment, beat the sugar and butter on medium speed until light and fluffy, 4 to 5 minutes, scraping down the bottom and sides of the bowl often. Reduce the speed to medium-low and gradually add the egg mixture a bit at a time, letting it fully incorporate before adding more and scraping down the bowl and beater as needed. ⟶

◆ Reduce the speed to low and add the flour mixture in three additions, alternating with two additions of the milk, mixing until just combined and scraping down the bowl as needed. Use a silicone spatula to fold the batter a few more times to make sure it's smooth.

◆ Divide the batter evenly between the prepared pans and smooth out the tops. Bake, rotating and switching their positions halfway through, until the cakes spring back when pressed and a tester inserted into the centers comes out clean, 25 to 30 minutes. Transfer the pans to a wire rack and allow the cakes to cool completely. (The frosting is best used as soon as it's made, so the cakes should be fully cooled and leveled if needed before proceeding.)

◆ To make the frosting, in a small bowl, whisk together the malted milk powder and brown sugar so there aren't any lumps; top with the chocolate. In a small saucepan, heat the heavy cream over medium heat until the edges begin to simmer. Pour the hot cream over the chocolate and let it sit, undisturbed, for 1 minute. Whisk until the mixture comes together and is smooth and shiny. Allow it to cool to room temperature—if you're strapped for time, chill it in the freezer, stirring every few minutes, until it is cool to the touch, 10 to 15 minutes.

◆ Meanwhile, in the bowl of a stand mixer fitted with the paddle attachment, beat the butter on medium-high speed until light and fluffy, 2 to 3 minutes. Sift in the powdered sugar, then add the vanilla and salt. Mix on low speed to combine, then increase the speed to medium-high and beat until light and fluffy, 2 to 3 minutes. Add the cooled ganache and mix on low speed to fully incorporate, pausing to scrape down the bowl. Increase the speed to medium and beat until light, fluffy, and silky, 45 to 60 seconds. Season with more salt to taste. For the best consistency, use immediately. Otherwise refrigerate in an airtight container for up to 2 weeks—allow it to come to room temperature and re-whip before using.

◆ To assemble the cake (see pages 94–95), place one of the layers (top side up) on a cake stand or plate. Tuck strips of parchment paper under the edge of the cake to keep the plate clean. Top the layer with about 1 cup of the frosting and use an offset spatula to spread it into an even layer. Center the second cake layer (top side down) over the frosted layer and nestle it on top. Using as little frosting as possible, spread a very thin crumb coat over the top and sides of the cake and fill any gaps. If possible, refrigerate the cake for 20 minutes to set it.

◆ Spread the remaining frosting evenly all over the top and sides of the cake, making swoops and swirls with the spatula or a spoon. Serve the cake the same day or refrigerate for 2 to 3 days—allow it to come to room temperature before serving.

VARIATION: To make a chocolate birthday cake, follow the Fudgy Devil's Food Sheet Cake recipe but bake in two greased and parchment-lined 8- or 9-inch round pans for 30 to 35 minutes.

Square and Rectangular Cakes

BANANA CAKE, TWO WAYS

1⅓ cups (175 g) all-purpose flour
1 teaspoon baking powder
1 teaspoon kosher salt
¾ teaspoon baking soda
¾ teaspoon lightly packed freshly grated nutmeg
½ teaspoon ground cinnamon
1 cup (225 g) mashed ripe bananas (about 1½ to 2 bananas)
⅓ cup (80 g) sour cream
2 tablespoons neutral oil, such as canola or safflower
1½ teaspoons vanilla extract
½ cup (115 g) unsalted butter, at room temperature
½ cup (100 g) granulated sugar, plus more for sprinkling
⅓ cup (75 g) firmly packed light brown sugar
1 egg, at room temperature
¾ cup (85 g) toasted walnuts, chopped
2 ounces (55 g) milk or semisweet chocolate, chopped (about ½ cup)

Don't get me wrong, I love banana bread as much as the next person, but this light, fluffy cake has got my vote for best use of ripened bananas. I'm presenting you with two versions—one chockablock with chocolate and walnuts and a crisped sugar topping, and the other spread with a creamy peanut butter frosting. It's a choose-your-own-adventure type of dessert! Either way, this makes a perfect snacking cake that you'll return to for seconds . . . and thirds.

MAKES 9 TO 12 SERVINGS

WITHOUT FROSTING

◆ Preheat the oven to 350 degrees F. Grease an 8-inch square pan and line the bottom with parchment paper.

◆ In a small bowl, whisk together the flour, baking powder, salt, baking soda, nutmeg, and cinnamon. In a medium bowl, whisk together the mashed bananas, sour cream, oil, and vanilla until combined.

◆ In the bowl of a stand mixer fitted with the paddle attachment, beat the butter and both sugars on medium speed until light and fluffy, 4 to 5 minutes, scraping down the bottom and sides of the bowl as needed. Add the egg and beat to fully incorporate.

◆ Reduce the speed to low and add the flour mixture in three additions, alternating with two additions of the banana mixture, mixing until just combined and scraping down the bowl as needed. Fold in the walnuts and chocolate.

• Scrape the batter into the prepared pan and smooth out the top. Sprinkle with about 2 tablespoons granulated sugar. Bake until the cake starts to pull away slightly from the edges, looks a bit crackled on top, and a tester inserted into the center comes out clean, 30 to 40 minutes. Transfer the pan to a wire rack and allow the cake to cool completely.

• Serve warm or at room temperature. (I love to cut the cake into squares and top it with ice cream and chocolate fudge for a killer sundae.) This cake keeps well wrapped at room temperature for 3 to 4 days.

WITH FROSTING

½ cup (130 g) creamy peanut butter (not natural)
6 tablespoons (85 g) unsalted butter, at room temperature
2 tablespoons honey
⅓ cup (40 g) powdered sugar
½ teaspoon vanilla extract
¼ teaspoon kosher salt
2 tablespoons roasted salted peanuts, chopped, for garnish (optional)

To make the frosted version, omit the chopped chocolate and walnuts from the batter, and forgo the crisped sugar topping. Bake and cool the cake as directed, then spread this peanut butter frosting over the top and, if you like, garnish with roasted salted peanuts.

• In the bowl of a stand mixer fitted with the paddle attachment, beat the peanut butter, butter, and honey on medium speed until light, fluffy, and smooth, 2 to 3 minutes. Sift in the powdered sugar, and add the vanilla and salt to taste. Mix on low speed to combine, then increase the speed to medium and continue beating until light and creamy, another 2 to 3 minutes. The frosting can be used immediately or refrigerated for up to 1 week.

BROWNED BUTTER HAZELNUT CAKE WITH SUGARED PLUMS

½ cup plus 1 tablespoon (125 g) unsalted butter
1⅓ cups plus 1 tablespoon (140 g) hazelnut flour (see Note)
¾ cup plus 1 tablespoon (100 g) powdered sugar
⅓ cup (65 g) granulated sugar
⅓ cup (45 g) spelt flour or all-purpose flour, plus more for dusting
¾ teaspoon kosher salt
Generous ½ cup (140 g) egg whites (from 4 to 5 eggs), at room temperature
1 teaspoon vanilla extract, or ½ teaspoon almond extract
Whipped cream, for serving

For the sugared plums
12 ounces (340 g) ripe yet firm plums, halved and pitted
1 tablespoon granulated sugar
Splash of kirsch or brandy (optional)
Pinch of kosher salt
Pinch of freshly ground black pepper (optional)

This easy-to-make cake is essentially one large *financier*—a bite-size French pastry that, when baked in its traditional small rectangular mold, resembles a bar of gold. Just eight simple ingredients are all that's needed, and the result is nothing short of delectable, with its chewy edges and rich crumb. While you can use ground almond or even pistachio here, I opt for hazelnut flour for the way it amplifies the toasty browned butter and adds a hint of cocoa. Lightly sweet and similarly nutty spelt flour further amplifies those flavors. Eat the cake plain or dress it up with macerated or roasted fruit and a dollop of whipped cream. Here I pair it with plums—their tangy sweet-sour flavor marries well with hazelnut.

MAKES 9 TO 12 SERVINGS

◆ Preheat the oven to 375 degrees F. Grease an 8-inch square pan and dust the inside with flour.

◆ Melt the butter in a small saucepan with a light-colored bottom (this will make it easier to check browning) over medium heat. The butter will foam and start to vigorously bubble. Continue cooking at a low simmer, swirling the pan occasionally, until the bubbling subsides and the butter begins to brown and smell nutty. Remove from the heat and allow the butter to keep browning in the pan—the aim is a golden caramel color.

NOTE: You can also make the cake batter in a food processor if you only have whole nuts: process a heaping 1 cup (140 g) nuts with the dry ingredients until finely ground. Add the egg whites and vanilla and pulse to combine, then pulse in the butter while adding it in a thin stream. Proceed with baking as instructed.

◆ In a large bowl, whisk together the hazelnut flour, both sugars, spelt flour, and salt. Use your fingers to break apart any clumps. In a medium bowl, whisk the egg whites vigorously by hand until frothy. Whisk the whites and the vanilla into the dry ingredients. Gradually pour in the warm browned butter, whisking to incorporate before adding more. Be sure to get all the browned bits from the pan. At this point, the batter can be refrigerated for up to 1 day before baking.

◆ Scrape the batter into the prepared pan and rap it against the countertop a few times to spread it out evenly. Bake until the cake is golden brown and a tester inserted into the center comes out clean, 25 to 30 minutes. Transfer the pan to a wire rack to cool.

◆ While the cake is baking, make the sugared plums. In a medium bowl, toss the fruit with the sugar, kirsch, salt, and pepper. Let sit for 20 to 30 minutes, tossing occasionally, to draw out the juices. Add more sugar to taste.

◆ Serve the cake warm or at room temperature, topping each piece with a dollop of whipped cream and a spoonful of plums. This cake keeps well wrapped at room temperature for 4 to 5 days.

"GRATED" JAM CAKE

2¼ cups *minus* 1 tablespoon (285 g) all-purpose flour, plus ½ cup (65 g) for grated topping
2 teaspoons baking powder
1¼ teaspoons kosher salt
1 teaspoon ground ginger (optional)
1 cup (225 g) unsalted butter, at room temperature
1 cup (200 g) granulated sugar
2 eggs, at room temperature
1¼ teaspoons vanilla extract
1 cup (335 g) jam or preserves, such as sour cherry, black or red currant, apricot, or a blend
¼ cup (40 g) crystallized ginger, finely chopped (optional)
⅓ cup (35 g) sliced almonds
Powdered sugar, for dusting

This Russian dessert is called *tyerti pirog*, literally "grated cake," for the way you grate a portion of the dough over the jam layer. The bottom has a melt-in-your-mouth, shortbread-like texture, while the grated topping is a nice crunchy counterpoint. The cake is also a great way to use up any surplus jam or preserves. I like to blend tart preserves, like sour cherry or red or black currant, with something a bit sweeter, like apricot or strawberry. While the optional ginger here is not traditional, I find it adds a nuanced pop of flavor.

MAKES 9 TO 12 SERVINGS

✦ Grease an 8-inch square pan and line the bottom with parchment paper.

✦ In a medium bowl, whisk together the 2¼ cups *minus* 1 tablespoon (285 g) flour, baking powder, salt, and ginger.

✦ In the bowl of a stand mixer fitted with the paddle attachment, beat the butter and sugar on medium speed until light and fluffy, 4 to 5 minutes, scraping down the bottom and sides of the bowl often. Add the eggs one at a time, beating to fully incorporate after each addition and scraping down the bowl as needed. Add the vanilla and mix to combine. ⟶

• Reduce the speed to low and add the flour mixture in two batches, mixing until just combined and scraping down the bowl as needed. Spoon three-quarters of the batter (about 620 g) into the prepared pan and use an offset spatula to spread the thick batter out evenly. Set aside. To the batter left in the mixer bowl, add the remaining ½ cup (65 g) flour and mix on low speed to combine. Pat the dough into a disk and freeze until thoroughly chilled, 45 to 60 minutes.

• When ready to bake, preheat the oven to 350 degrees F. Use an offset spatula or spoon to spread the jam over the batter in the pan. Use a box grater to evenly grate half of the chilled dough over the cake. Sprinkle with the crystallized ginger. Evenly grate the remaining dough over the top—do not press it down.

• Bake the cake until the top begins to brown, about 35 minutes. Remove from the oven and distribute the almonds evenly over the top. Return to the oven and bake until golden brown and a tester inserted into the center comes out clean, another 10 to 15 minutes. Allow to cool to warm or room temperature before dusting with powdered sugar. Cut into squares and serve. The squares keep well wrapped at room temperature for 3 or 4 days.

FROSTED APPLE-CINNAMON OAT CAKE

1⅓ cups plus 2 tablespoons (185 g) all-purpose flour

½ cup (40 g) quick-cooking oats (see Note)

1½ teaspoons baking powder

1½ teaspoons ground cinnamon

1 teaspoon kosher salt

½ teaspoon lightly packed freshly grated nutmeg or ground cloves

¼ teaspoon baking soda

⅔ cup (130 g) refined coconut oil, at room temperature (see Note)

½ cup (100 g) granulated sugar

½ cup (100 g) packed light brown sugar

2 eggs, at room temperature

1½ teaspoons vanilla extract

1½ cups (225 g) grated unpeeled apples

1 cup (115 g) diced unpeeled apples

¾ cup (75 g) toasted pecans or walnuts, chopped

Baked apple chips, whole or lightly crushed, for topping (optional)

CONTINUED

This soon-to-be-your-favorite fall cake gets a triple dose of apple. The fruit is both grated and diced for textural contrast and maximal flavor. Sparkling cider makes a slightly tart and silky-smooth frosting, and a final scattering of baked apple chips (I like the Bare brand) leaves things extra pretty. Oats, spices, and nuts accentuate the autumn vibe. For a humbler (and dairy-free!) treat, omit the frosting and garnish. Avoid apples that are soft and tend to fall apart when baking, like McIntosh, Gala, and Fuji.

MAKES 9 TO 12 SERVINGS

◆ Preheat the oven to 350 degrees F. Grease an 8-inch square pan and line the bottom with parchment paper.

◆ In a medium bowl, whisk together the flour, oats, baking powder, cinnamon, salt, nutmeg, and baking soda.

◆ In the bowl of a stand mixer fitted with the paddle attachment, beat the coconut oil and both sugars on medium speed until light and relatively fluffy, 4 to 5 minutes. Add the eggs one at a time, beating to fully incorporate after each addition and scraping down the bowl as needed. Add the vanilla and mix to combine.

◆ Reduce the speed to low and add the flour mixture in two batches, mixing until just combined and scraping down the bowl as needed. Mix in the diced and grated apples (along with any juices) and pecans. Use a spatula to scrape down the bowl once more and fold the batter a few times to make sure it's evenly combined. ⟶

For the frosting

½ cup (120 ml) nonalcoholic sparkling apple cider or no-sugar-added apple juice

2½ tablespoons all-purpose flour

⅓ cup (65 g) granulated sugar

½ teaspoon vanilla extract

¼ teaspoon kosher salt

½ cup (115 g) unsalted butter, at room temperature

NOTE: If you only have old-fashioned oats, you can pulse them in a food processor 5 to 10 times to make them quick-cooking oats.

At room temperature, coconut oil remains solid, resulting in a rich, yet buttery crumb—substitute with another neutral oil if you don't have it.

♦ Scrape the batter into the prepared pan and smooth out the top. Bake until the top is golden brown, the sides begin to pull away from the pan, and a tester inserted into the center comes out clean, 35 to 45 minutes. Transfer the pan to a wire rack and allow the cake to cool completely.

♦ To make the frosting, in a small saucepan, whisk the apple cider and flour together until smooth and lump-free. Whisking constantly, cook over medium heat until the mixture turns into a thick, pudding-like paste, 2 to 3 minutes. Remove from the heat and whisk in the sugar, vanilla, and salt. Let the mixture cool to room temperature (you can pop it into the refrigerator to speed this up).

♦ In the bowl of a stand mixer fitted with the paddle attachment, beat the butter on medium-high speed until light and fluffy, 3 to 4 minutes, scraping down the bowl often. Reduce the speed to medium and add the cooled cider mixture a large spoonful at a time. Once all the mixture has been added, scrape down the bowl once more, then increase the speed to medium-high. Beat until the frosting is silky-smooth, light, and fluffy, 3 to 4 minutes. Season with more vanilla or salt to taste. Use the frosting immediately or refrigerate in an airtight container for up to 1 week. Allow it to come to room temperature and re-whip before using.

♦ Scrape the frosting onto the center of the cooled cake and smooth it out in an even layer. Top with the baked apple chips. The unfrosted cake keeps well wrapped at room temperature for 3 to 4 days. Once frosted, the cake can be kept at room temperature for 1 day before it needs to be refrigerated, at which point it will keep for another 2 to 3 days.

FRENCH CUSTARD CAKE

¾ cup (100 g) all-purpose flour
⅔ cup (135 g) granulated sugar
½ teaspoon kosher salt
5 eggs
1 cup (235 ml) heavy cream
1 cup (235 ml) whole milk (see Note)
2 tablespoons brandy, cognac, rum, kirsch, calvados, or other eau-de-vie
2 teaspoons vanilla extract
1 to 1¼ pounds (about 3 cups) cherries, fresh berries, rhubarb, plums, peaches, apples, or pears

For assembly
Unsalted butter, for greasing
Granulated sugar, for dusting and topping
Powdered sugar, for dusting (optional)

France has a myriad of fruit-baked-in-custard cakes: clafouti with cherries, *far normand* with apples, *flaugnarde* with pears, and *far breton* with plumped prunes or other dried fruit. This custard cake is none of these, but certainly inspired by all. The rich, booze-spiked batter comes together in seconds in a blender and lends itself to being baked year-round with any seasonal fruit—or vegetable, in the case of rhubarb—you might have on hand, though do avoid anything too juicy or overly ripe. It's an effortless dessert that will impress any guest. So very French!

MAKES 8 TO 10 SERVINGS

⁕ In a blender, blend all of the ingredients on medium speed until the batter is completely smooth and lump-free, 20 to 45 seconds depending on your blender. Alternatively, in a large bowl, whisk together the flour, sugar, and salt. Add the eggs and whisk until smooth. Whisk in the cream, milk, brandy, and vanilla. Chill the batter in the refrigerator for at least 1 hour or in an airtight container for up to 3 days.

⁕ Meanwhile, prep your chosen fruit: pit cherries; trim and cut rhubarb into 1-inch pieces and toss with 1 to 2 tablespoons sugar; pit and thickly slice plums or peaches. If using apples or pears, prep and cook according to the sidebar on page 110. You will need 3 cups prepped fruit for the cake.

⁕ To assemble, first preheat the oven to 350 degrees F. Generously butter a deep 2-quart baking dish—such as one 11 by 7 inches or a 9-inch square—and lightly coat with granulated sugar. Tap out any excess. ⟶

• Stir the batter to reincorporate any flour that has settled to the bottom. Arrange the fruit in an even layer in the baking dish, and if using apples or pears, reserve some for the top. Slowly pour the batter over the fruit, making sure not to disturb it too much. Top with the remaining fruit and sprinkle evenly with 3 tablespoons granulated sugar.

• Bake until the cake puffs up, is a nice golden color, and a tester inserted into the center comes out relatively clean, 55 to 70 minutes. Don't be alarmed if the cake sinks as it cools—this is normal. Dust with powdered sugar and serve warm or at room temperature. This cake is best the day it is baked but will keep well wrapped in the refrigerator for up to 1 day.

USING APPLES OR PEARS

To prep apples or pears, peel, core, and slice them ⅛ inch thick. In a medium bowl, toss the slices with 2 tablespoons granulated sugar and ¼ teaspoon kosher salt. Heat a large skillet over medium heat. Add the fruit and cook, stirring often, until it begins to soften and release juices and the edges start to turn translucent, 3 to 5 minutes. The centers should still have a bit of crunch. Remove from the heat. Add ¼ cup of whichever liquor you've used in the batter and toss to combine. Let the mixture cool to room temperature before proceeding with assembly.

GOLDEN-MILK TRES LECHES CAKE

6 eggs, at room temperature
  (see Note)
1 cup (200 g) granulated sugar
1 teaspoon vanilla extract
1⅓ cups (175 g) all-purpose
  flour
3 tablespoons cornstarch
1½ teaspoons baking powder
¾ teaspoon kosher salt
3 tablespoons neutral oil,
  such as canola or safflower

For the tres leches
1 (13.5-ounce) can light
  coconut milk
1½ cups (355 ml) whole milk
2 teaspoons vanilla bean
  paste or extract
1½ teaspoons ground turmeric
1¼ teaspoons ground ginger
½ teaspoon lightly packed
  freshly grated nutmeg
½ teaspoon kosher salt
4 to 5 whole black peppercorns
3 cardamom pods, crushed,
  or ½ teaspoon ground
  cardamom
1 cinnamon stick, or ½ teaspoon ground cinnamon
1 (14-ounce) can sweetened
  condensed milk

For the whipped cream
2 cups (475 ml) cold heavy
  cream
2 tablespoons honey or
  granulated sugar
Ground cinnamon, for dusting

This Latin American dessert consists of a sponge cake soaked through with tres leches (Spanish for "three milks") and then topped with whipped cream. For a twist, the tres leches here begins as golden milk—a traditional Indian drink that has its roots in Ayurveda. Infused with turmeric, ginger, cinnamon, and other spices, this electric-yellow tres leches marries two vibrant cuisines into one irresistible cake.

Don't skimp on the whipped cream—it helps cut the sweetness and makes each bite extra creamy.

MAKES 12 TO 16 SERVINGS

✦ Preheat the oven to 350 degrees F. Line the bottom of a 9-by-13-inch glass or ceramic baking dish with parchment paper.

✦ In the bowl of a stand mixer fitted with the whisk attachment, beat the eggs and sugar on medium-high speed until thick ribbons form (see page 42), about 10 minutes. Add the vanilla and mix to combine. Meanwhile, in a medium bowl, sift together the flour, cornstarch, baking powder, and salt.

✦ Use a silicone spatula to gently but confidently fold one-third of the flour mixture into the egg mixture by hand. Repeat with the rest of the flour mixture in two batches—be careful not to overmix! Drizzle in the oil and fold to thoroughly combine.

✦ Gently scrape the batter into the prepared dish and gently smooth out the top. Bake the cake until it springs back when pressed and a tester inserted into the center comes out clean, 30 to 35 minutes. Transfer the pan to a wire rack and allow the cake to cool completely. ⟶

• Meanwhile, make the tres leches. In a medium saucepan, whisk together all the ingredients except for the sweetened condensed milk. Bring to a simmer over medium-high heat. Reduce the heat, and gently simmer for 3 minutes. Remove from the heat, cover, and let steep for 1 hour, or until the cake has cooled. Remove the cinnamon stick and whisk in the sweetened condensed milk. At this point, I like to transfer the tres leches to a large liquid measuring cup or small pitcher for easy pouring.

• Once the cake is cool, run a knife around the edges of the pan and invert it onto a cutting board. Remove the parchment from the cake and flip it over again. Use a serrated knife to cut off the cake's browned top—you may be able to simply peel it off. This extra step ensures that the cake will be evenly soaked through. Nestle the cake (cut side up) back into the baking dish. Gradually pour the tres leches evenly over the top. Remove any cardamom shells or peppercorns that have fallen onto the cake. Allow to sit at room temperature for 30 minutes, then cover and refrigerate for at least 6 hours and ideally overnight.

• Up to a few hours before serving, make the whipped cream. In the bowl of a stand mixer fitted with the whisk attachment, whip the heavy cream and honey on medium-high speed until it holds stiff peaks. Spread it evenly over the top of the cake and lightly dust with cinnamon.

• Serve immediately or refrigerate until ready to serve. This cake keeps well in the refrigerator for up to 4 days.

SUMMER BERRY BUCKLE WITH CRUNCHY SUGAR

½ cup (115 g) unsalted butter
¼ cup (60 ml) heavy cream
4½ cups (about 18 ounces)
  mixed fresh or frozen
  berries, such as blueberries,
  raspberries, and
  blackberries (see Note)
2½ cups (300 g) cake flour,
  sifted, or 1¾ cups (245 g)
  all-purpose flour, plus more
  for tossing (see Note)
3 eggs, at room temperature
1½ cups (300 g) granulated
  sugar, divided
Finely grated zest of 1 large
  lemon (about 1 to 1½
  tablespoons)
2 teaspoons baking powder
1½ teaspoons vanilla extract
¾ teaspoon kosher salt
2 tablespoons freshly
  squeezed lemon juice or
  water
Ice cream or whipped cream,
  for serving

This recipe was originally published in *Gourmet* magazine in 2000. My mom somehow obtained a clipping of the recipe, and I'm glad she did because twenty years later, it's still one of our favorite summer cakes. I've since adapted it—adding a crackly sugar topping and reducing the quantity of berries. Don't worry, though, it's still bursting with fruit. So much so that I've dubbed it a buckle, from the way the batter buckles under the weight of the berries. It's highly snackable and travels well, so pack it up for a picnic, the beach, or a summer barbecue.

The "snowy" sugar topping, adapted from Shauna Sever's *Midwest Made*, doesn't dissolve into the batter and adds a fun effect to the surface as well as a welcome crunch to each bite.

MAKES 12 SERVINGS

◆ Preheat the oven to 350 degrees F. Grease a 9-by-13-inch pan. If you're not planning to serve the cake from the pan, line the bottom with parchment paper.

◆ In a small saucepan, warm the butter and heavy cream over low heat until the butter melts. Set aside to cool. In a medium bowl, toss the berries with 2 teaspoons flour to lightly coat.

◆ In the bowl of a stand mixer fitted with the whisk attachment, beat the eggs and 1 cup (200 g) of the sugar on high speed until thick ribbons form (see page 42), 6 to 8 minutes. Reduce the speed to low and add the lemon zest, baking

powder, vanilla, and salt; mix to combine. Pause the mixer and
add half of the flour and half of the cooled butter. Mix on low
speed until incorporated, scraping down the bottom and sides
of the bowl as needed. Add the remaining flour and butter
mixture and beat on medium speed until the batter is thick
and sticky, 30 to 45 seconds. Use a silicone spatula to gently
fold in the berries until just combined.

◆ Dollop the batter evenly into the prepared pan and use a
spatula or the back of a spoon to carefully smooth out in an
even layer without crushing the berries too much. Put the
remaining ½ cup (100 g) sugar into one small bowl and the
lemon juice into a second. Dip your fingertips into the lemon
juice and work them through the sugar to make it clump
slightly, like snow (you might have to dip your fingers one or
two more times). Evenly top the cake with the snowy sugar.

◆ Bake until the top is golden, the berries begin to bubble
slightly, and a tester inserted into the center of the cake
comes out clean, 45 to 55 minutes. Transfer the pan to a wire
rack and serve the cake warm or at room temperature with ice
cream or slightly sweetened whipped cream. This cake keeps
well wrapped at room temperature for 3 to 4 days.

SANTINA'S TIRAMISU

6 eggs, separated, at room temperature

¼ cup (50 g) granulated sugar

½ cup (100 g) packed light brown sugar

2⅔ cups (600 g) mascarpone, at room temperature

½ cup (120 ml) Cointreau, brandy, rum, marsala wine, or Kahlúa, divided

2 cups (475 ml) very strong brewed coffee or good espresso, at room temperature

1 (14-ounce) package ladyfingers, or 2 (14.5-ounce) packages Italian milk-and-honey biscuits (see page 120)

About 1 ounce semisweet or bittersweet chocolate, for grating

Cocoa powder, for dusting

When I was twenty-three, I went on a six-week-long tour through Europe, and while in northern Italy, I met a lovely woman named Santina through a friend I was staying with. She taught me how to make tiramisu—a layered dessert of booze-spiked mascarpone cream and coffee-soaked ladyfingers (or in Santina's case, biscuits—see page 120). Even before she had finished assembling the dessert, I knew it would be my most treasured souvenir from that trip. With her permission, I share it here, albeit with a few changes I've made over the years. I hope it transports you to Italy like it does me.

MAKES 12 TO 16 SERVINGS

◆ In the bowl of a stand mixer fitted with the whisk attachment, whip the egg whites on medium speed until soft peaks form (see page 51). Gradually add the granulated sugar and continue to whip until firm peaks form. Transfer the meringue to a different bowl and set aside.

◆ In the same bowl (no need to wash!), beat the egg yolks and brown sugar on high speed, scraping down the bottom and sides of the bowl as needed, until thick ribbons form (see page 42), 6 to 8 minutes. Reduce the speed to low and add the mascarpone, mixing until no lumps remain. Add ¼ cup (60 ml) of the Cointreau and beat to just combine. Using a silicone spatula, gently fold one-third of the meringue into the mascarpone until just combined. Gently fold in the remaining meringue. Set aside. ⟶

NOTE: For an extra thick and voluminous mascarpone cream, whip ¾ cup (175 ml) cold heavy cream until firm peaks form, then fold it into the mascarpone mixture after the meringue is added.

◆ In a medium shallow bowl, combine the coffee and remaining ¼ cup (60 ml) Cointreau. One at a time, place a ladyfinger into the coffee, then quickly roll it over to soak the other side—this shouldn't take more than 3 seconds. Transfer the ladyfinger to a deep 9-by-13-inch or a standard 11-by-15-inch glass or ceramic dish. Repeat with enough soaked ladyfingers to make a single layer of three rows, trimming them to fit if necessary. Spread with half of the mascarpone cream. Finely grate an even layer of chocolate over the top.

◆ Dip the remaining ladyfingers in coffee and arrange another three-row layer over the mascarpone. Spread the remaining mascarpone on top. Cover and chill for at least 6 hours and ideally overnight. Remove the dish from the refrigerator 30 minutes before serving. Dust evenly with cocoa powder and finely grate more chocolate over the top. This cake keeps well covered in the refrigerator for 3 to 4 days.

TIRAMISU WITH BISCUIT COOKIES

While ladyfingers are traditional, Santina makes her tiramisu with *novellini*—Italian milk-and-honey biscuit cookies that maintain a nice texture while still soaking up and carrying the boozy-coffee flavor. You can find them at Italian specialty shops and, to my delight, Trader Joe's, where they are labeled as Lattemiele. When using biscuits, follow the recipe as written but create more tiramisu layers: four of coffee-soaked biscuits and three of mascarpone cream. Dunk the biscuits into the coffee completely but quickly—no more than 2 seconds—to prevent them from disintegrating.

CONFETTI CAKE WITH STRAWBERRY FROSTING

2½ cups (300 g) cake flour, sifted, or 2 cups (260 g) all-purpose flour
¼ cup (30 g) cornstarch (omit if using cake flour)
2 teaspoons baking powder
1¼ teaspoons kosher salt
1⅓ cups (265 g) granulated sugar
¾ cup (170 g) unsalted butter, at room temperature
4 egg whites, at room temperature
2 tablespoons neutral oil, such as canola or safflower
2½ teaspoons vanilla extract
⅔ cup (160 ml) buttermilk, at room temperature
½ cup (80 g) rainbow sprinkles, plus more for sprinkling

For the frosting
¾ ounce freeze-dried strawberries (heaping ¾ cup)
1½ cups (340 g) unsalted butter, at room temperature
3 cups (360 g) powdered sugar
3 tablespoons whole milk, at room temperature
1 tablespoon vanilla extract
¾ teaspoon apple cider vinegar
¾ teaspoon kosher salt

If you ever attended a birthday party as a kid, then inevitably you came across a confetti cake. Studded with bright pops of color (hello, sprinkles!), it's almost always topped with an American buttercream. Because it lacks egg yolks, this white cake is soft and tender and a perfect backdrop for confetti. Don't miss the pink-hued frosting—it tastes just like strawberry ice cream thanks to freeze-dried strawberries. Truly a cake that everyone will line up for.

If you don't have cake flour, all-purpose flour and cornstarch mimic it to ensure a light crumb. When choosing sprinkles, artificially colored long rainbow sprinkles or confetti quins (little discs) work best here; the nonpareils-style (little balls) tends to bleed.

MAKES 12 TO 16 SERVINGS

• Preheat the oven to 350 degrees F. Grease a 9-by-13-inch pan and line the bottom with parchment paper.

• In a medium bowl, sift together the flour, cornstarch (if using), baking powder, and salt.

• In the bowl of a stand mixer fitted with the paddle attachment, beat the sugar and butter on medium speed until light and fluffy, 4 to 5 minutes, scraping down the bottom and sides of the bowl as needed. Add the egg whites one at a time, mixing until the batter is combined and lump-free and scraping down the bowl and paddle after each addition. Add the oil and vanilla and mix to combine. ⟶

NOTE: While this recipe is written for a 9-by-13-inch pan, you can also bake it in two greased and parchment-lined 8-inch round or square pans for a layer cake; the baking time for two pans will be about 25 minutes. You will need to make one and a half batches of frosting. The batter can also be halved to make a smaller single layer. If you omit the strawberry powder in the frosting, you'll still have a very good vanilla butter-cream base that you can use plain or play around with.

• Add the flour mixture in three additions, alternating with two additions of the buttermilk, mixing until just combined and scraping down the bowl as needed. Use a silicone spatula to fold in the sprinkles and make sure the batter is smooth and fully combined.

• Scrape the batter into the prepared pan and smooth out the top. Bake the cake until a tester inserted into the center comes out clean, 25 to 30 minutes. Transfer the pan to a wire rack and allow the cake to cool completely.

• To make the frosting, pulse the strawberries in a food processor until finely ground. Use immediately or store in an airtight container for up to 3 months. In the bowl of a stand mixer fitted with the paddle attachment, beat the butter on medium speed until it has a soft, spreadable consistency, about 2 minutes. Sift in the powdered sugar and add the milk, vanilla, vinegar, and salt. Beat on the lowest speed for a full 3 to 4 minutes, until the frosting is smooth and creamy but not light and fluffy. Add the strawberry powder and beat to combine. The frosting should be used immediately or transferred to an airtight container and refrigerated for up to 2 weeks. Bring it to room temperature and re-whip on low speed until smooth and creamy before using.

• To assemble, scrape the frosting onto the cooled cake and use an offset spatula to smooth it out in an even layer. Top with sprinkles, then cut into squares and serve. This cake is best on the day it is baked but will keep covered at room temperature for up to 1 day or in the refrigerator for up to 5 days. Bring to room temperature before serving.

FUDGY DEVIL'S FOOD SHEET CAKE

¾ cup (75 g) Dutch-process cocoa powder

1 ounce (28 g) unsweetened chocolate, finely chopped

1 cup (235 ml) very hot freshly brewed coffee

2 cups (260 g) all-purpose flour

1 cup plus 2 tablespoons (225 g) firmly packed dark brown sugar

1 cup (200 g) granulated sugar

1½ teaspoons kosher salt

1 teaspoon baking soda

1 teaspoon baking powder

2 eggs, at room temperature

1 cup (235 ml) buttermilk, at room temperature

½ cup (120 ml) neutral oil, such as canola or safflower

1½ teaspoons vanilla extract

For a brief time in college, I had a small bake-to-order "business," where I took orders for cakes, cookies, brownies, you name it. It was short-lived (the numbers, I quickly realized, didn't quite add up), but even so, I managed to squeak out a best seller: this easy-to-make chocolate cake. I've since tinkered with it—adding buttermilk and using unsweetened chocolate, cocoa powder, and freshly brewed coffee to coax out a rich, deep chocolate flavor. The thick, fudgy frosting has all the nostalgic vibes and turns this cake into an instant crowd-pleaser that my college self would be proud to serve. In place of the brewed coffee in the batter, you can swap 1 cup (235 ml) very hot water and 1½ teaspoons espresso powder (add the latter with the cocoa powder), or omit the espresso powder completely—the chocolate flavor will be just a little less pronounced.

MAKES 12 TO 16 SERVINGS

◆ Preheat the oven to 350 degrees F. Grease a 9-by-13-inch pan and line the bottom with parchment paper.

◆ In a medium bowl, stir together the cocoa powder and chopped chocolate. Pour the hot coffee over the top and stir until the cocoa has dissolved and the chocolate has completely melted. Set aside to cool.

◆ Meanwhile, in a large bowl, whisk together the flour, both sugars, salt, baking soda, and baking powder. Use your fingers to break up any lumps. Add the eggs, buttermilk, oil, vanilla, and cooled chocolate mixture and whisk to combine until smooth and glossy.

For the frosting

2⅔ cups (320 g) powdered sugar

½ cup (50 g) Dutch-process or other unsweetened cocoa powder

½ teaspoon instant espresso powder (optional)

Rounded ¼ teaspoon kosher salt

½ cup (115 g) unsalted butter, at room temperature

⅓ cup (80 ml) boiling water

1½ ounces (45 g) unsweetened chocolate, melted

½ teaspoon vanilla extract

Sprinkles or flaky sea salt, for sprinkling (optional)

✦ Scrape the batter into the prepared pan and bake until the cake is matte and firm and a tester inserted into the center comes out clean, 35 to 40 minutes. Transfer the pan to a wire rack and allow the cake to cool completely.

✦ To make the frosting, in the bowl of a stand mixer fitted with the paddle attachment, whisk together the powdered sugar, cocoa powder, espresso powder, and salt. Add the butter and boiling water and mix on low speed to combine. Increase the speed to medium and mix for 1 minute, or until the frosting is glossy and smooth, scraping down the bowl as needed. Add the melted chocolate and vanilla and mix to combine. Refrigerate for 30 minutes to firm before using. The frosting can be stored in an airtight container in the refrigerator for 4 to 5 days. Bring it to room temperature before using.

✦ To assemble, scrape the frosting onto the cooled cake and use an offset spatula to smooth it out in an even layer. Top with sprinkles or sea salt. Cut into squares and serve. This cake keeps well wrapped at room temperature for 3 to 4 days.

NOTE: While this recipe is written for a 9-by-13-inch pan, you can also bake it in two greased and parchment-lined 8- or 9-inch round or square pans for a layer cake; the baking time for two pans will be 30 to 35 minutes. You will need to make one and a half batches of frosting. The batter can also be halved to make a smaller single layer when you're simply craving a little chocolate cake.

SALTED BUTTERSCOTCH FUDGE SHEET CAKE

1 cup (235 ml) buttermilk,
at room temperature
1 cup (240 g) sour cream,
at room temperature
2 cups (400 g) granulated
sugar
2/3 cup (160 ml) neutral oil,
such as canola or safflower
5 tablespoons (70 g) unsalted
butter, at room temperature
4 teaspoons baking powder
2 teaspoons kosher salt
2 teaspoons vanilla extract
4 eggs, at room temperature
2¾ cups (360 g) all-purpose
flour
2 cups (230 g) toasted pecans,
chopped, for topping
Flaky sea salt, for topping
(optional)

For the icing
1½ cups (300 g) packed dark
brown sugar
¾ cup (170 g) unsalted butter
1½ teaspoons kosher salt
2/3 cup (160 ml) heavy cream
4 cups (480 g) powdered
sugar, sifted
1½ teaspoons vanilla extract

Sheet cakes are my go-to when I need to make dessert for a crowd—especially since the baking pan also functions as a serving vessel. Taking inspiration from both Texas sheet and Southern caramel cakes, this pillowy number tastes like a Werther's Original melted onto a cake. While you might raise an eyebrow at the amount of salt that goes into the icing, it's warranted; not only does it bring out the butterscotch flavor, it also keeps the sweetness in check.

MAKES 20 TO 24 SERVINGS

◆ Preheat the oven to 350 degrees F. Grease and line the bottom of a half-sheet (13-by-18-inch) pan with parchment paper.

◆ In a liquid measuring cup, whisk together the buttermilk and sour cream.

◆ In the bowl of a stand mixer fitted with the paddle attachment, beat the granulated sugar, oil, butter, baking powder, salt, and vanilla on low speed to combine. Increase the speed to medium and beat until the mixture has thickened and is smooth and white, about 2 minutes. With the mixer running, add the eggs one at a time, beating to fully incorporate after each addition and scraping down the bottom and sides of the bowl as needed.

◆ Reduce the speed to low and add the flour in two additions, mixing until just combined and scraping down the bowl after each addition. With the mixer running, gradually pour in the buttermilk mixture and mix until just incorporated. Scrape down the bowl and use a silicone spatula to fold the batter a few times to make sure it's smooth. $\longrightarrow$

• Scrape the batter into the prepared pan and smooth it out with an offset spatula. Bake the cake until lightly golden, puffed up, and a tester inserted into the center comes out clean, 25 to 35 minutes. Transfer to a wire rack to cool while you make the icing.

• To make the icing, in a medium heavy-bottomed saucepan, combine the brown sugar, butter, and salt (see Note). Cook over medium heat, stirring often, until the butter melts and the sugar dissolves. Continue stirring until the mixture comes together and starts to simmer at the edges. Once the first bubble in the center comes up, set a timer and cook, stirring constantly, for 2 minutes, or until a digital or candy thermometer registers 235 degrees F. Carefully pour in the heavy cream, and continue to cook, stirring often, for another 1½ minutes. At this point, the sauce should be slightly thickened and glossy. (Congrats, you've made butterscotch sauce!)

• Reduce the heat to low, then stir in the powdered sugar and vanilla. The icing will have clumps at first, but do your best using the back of a spoon to work them against the side of the pan. Working over low heat keeps the icing from hardening. It's OK if there are still some clumps left in the end—the pecans will hide them. The icing should be a thick, spreadable consistency.

• Have the pecans and sea salt at the ready. Remove the icing from the heat and immediately pour it over the center of the still-warm cake. Use an offset or silicone spatula to quickly distribute it evenly over the top. Try to do this in one fell swoop without too much fuss—the more you work the icing, the more it will crystallize and turn grainy, losing its shine. Immediately sprinkle the pecans and sea salt over the top.

• Allow the cake to completely cool before cutting it into squares and serving. This cake keeps well wrapped at room temperature for 3 to 4 days.

RUSSIAN NAPOLEON CAKE

1 (17.4-ounce) box frozen puff-pastry
2 cups (475 ml) whole milk
½ vanilla bean, split and scraped, or 1½ teaspoons vanilla bean paste or extract
½ teaspoon kosher salt
2 eggs
¾ cup (150 g) granulated sugar
2 tablespoons cornstarch
2 tablespoons all-purpose flour
¼ cup (55 g) unsalted butter, cut into 1-inch pieces
¾ cup (175 ml) cold heavy cream
Powdered sugar, for dusting

Originally brought to Russia in the nineteenth century from France, the Napoleon has become a classic dessert that Russians turn to for gatherings and celebrations. Many insist on letting the assembled cake sit in the fridge overnight for the layers to soften, but I prefer the textural contrast between flaky, crispy puff pastry and rich custard cream. That being said, I've never complained about refrigerated leftovers the next day with tea.

If you want more flaky layers, cut each unbaked pastry sheet in half crosswise, roll each piece into a roughly 10-by-14-inch rectangle, and dock all over with a fork. Bake one at a time for 10 to 12 minutes. Proceed as instructed.

MAKES 12 TO 16 SERVINGS

+ Preheat the oven to 375 degrees F. Lightly grease two half-sheet (13-by-18-inch) pans.

+ On a floured surface, unfold 1 puff pastry sheet (keep the other refrigerated). Lightly flour the top and a rolling pin to prevent sticking. Roll out the dough to roughly the size of the baking sheet and carefully transfer the dough onto the pan. Bake for 12 to 15 minutes, or until the puff pastry is firm and lightly golden. Allow the pastry to cool for a few minutes, then transfer it to a wire rack and allow the pastry to cool completely. Repeat with the second puff pastry sheet. The puff pastry can be baked up to a few hours in advance and kept at room temperature.

+ Meanwhile, make the pastry cream. In a medium saucepan, heat the milk, vanilla bean (if using), and salt over medium heat until it just barely comes to a boil. Remove from the heat and set aside. ⟶

◆ In a medium bowl, whisk together the eggs and sugar until the mixture pales in color and thickens. Add the cornstarch and flour, and whisk to fully incorporate. Gradually pour one-third of the hot milk into the egg mixture, 1 to 2 tablespoons at a time, whisking constantly as you do. Add the rest of the milk in a slow stream, whisking constantly. Return the mixture to the saucepan. Cook over medium-high heat, whisking the mixture until it thickens and starts to boil. Continue to cook, whisking constantly, for 3 full minutes to cook off the starch. The custard will have thickened significantly and will look glossy. Remove from the heat and transfer to a medium bowl. Whisk in the butter and vanilla extract (if using) until fully incorporated and the custard is smooth. Immediately place a piece of plastic wrap directly on the surface of the custard and chill in the refrigerator or at room temperature until completely cool.

◆ Once the pastry cream has cooled, whisk it thoroughly until softened and smoothed out. In the bowl of a stand mixer fitted with the whisk attachment, whip the heavy cream on medium-high speed until medium-soft peaks form. Gently fold one-third of the whipped cream into the pastry cream, then repeat with the remaining whipped cream in two batches. Use immediately or refrigerate for up to a few hours.

◆ To assemble, place the puff pastry sheets on top of each other on a large baking sheet and trim the edges with a serrated knife to give them a clean, even cut. Crumble the trimmings into a bowl and set aside. Place one pastry sheet on a serving platter. Spread a generous amount of pastry cream over the top. Top with the second sheet and spread that layer generously with pastry cream as well. Scatter the trimming crumbs over the top and dust with powdered sugar.

◆ Serve immediately or within 1 hour. This cake keeps well wrapped in the refrigerator for 2 to 3 days.

Loaf
Cakes

CANNOLI RICOTTA CAKE WITH CANDIED PISTACHIOS

1½ cups (195 g) all-purpose flour
2 teaspoons baking powder
1½ teaspoons instant espresso powder
1¼ teaspoons kosher salt
½ teaspoon ground cinnamon
1⅓ cups (320 g) whole-milk ricotta, at room temperature
1¼ cups (250 g) granulated sugar
¾ cup (170 g) unsalted butter, at room temperature
3 eggs, at room temperature
1½ teaspoons vanilla extract
½ cup (85 g) chopped homemade candied orange peel (recipe follows) or store-bought
⅓ cup (50 g) finely chopped bittersweet or semisweet chocolate

For the topping
⅓ to ½ cup (50 to 70 g) roasted shelled pistachios (see Note)
¼ cup (50 g) granulated sugar
2 tablespoons freshly squeezed orange juice
1 tablespoon freshly squeezed lemon juice
Pinch of kosher salt (if using unsalted pistachios)

This dessert pays homage to one of my favorite Italian treats: cannoli. If you haven't had the pleasure of eating one, it's a tube-shaped fried pastry dough shell filled with a sweet ricotta cream and then dipped in chopped pistachios, mini chocolate chips, or candied orange peel. I use all three to bring sparkle to this luscious and creamy ricotta pound cake. The chocolate and orange get folded into the batter, while the pistachios get quickly candied and serve as a glossy topping. If you have the time, try candying your own orange peel—it's worlds apart from the store-bought variety.

MAKES 6 TO 8 SERVINGS

• Preheat the oven to 350 degrees F. Grease a 9-by-5-inch loaf pan and line with parchment paper, leaving overhang on the long sides.

• In a small bowl, whisk together the flour, baking powder, espresso powder, salt, and cinnamon.

• In the bowl of a stand mixer fitted with the whisk attachment, beat the ricotta, sugar, and butter on medium speed until no lumps remain, 2 to 3 minutes. Add the eggs one at a time, beating to fully incorporate after each addition and scraping down the sides and bottom of the bowl as needed. The batter will look curdled. Add the vanilla and mix to combine. ⟶

• Reduce the speed to low and add the flour mixture in two additions, mixing just to combine and scraping down the bowl as needed. Gently fold in the candied orange and chopped chocolate.

• Scrape the batter into the prepared pan and use a spatula to smooth out the top. Bake until the cake begins to set and the edges begin to brown, 30 to 35 minutes. Loosely cover the pan with a piece of aluminum foil and continue baking until a tester inserted into the center of the cake comes out clean, another 30 to 40 minutes. Allow the cake to cool in the pan for 30 minutes before using the overhang to lift it out of the pan and transfer it to a wire rack. Cool completely before topping.

• To make the topping, combine the pistachios, sugar, citrus juices, and salt in a small saucepan and bring to a simmer over medium heat. Continue to simmer, stirring occasionally, until the syrup has thickened and turned glossy, 2 to 3 minutes. Immediately pour over the cooled cake and allow to set for 15 minutes before serving. The cake keeps well wrapped at room temperature for 3 to 4 days.

Candied Orange Peel

3 organic navel oranges, preferably with thick peels, rinsed well

2 cups (400 g) granulated sugar, divided

Domenica Marchetti is one of my favorite Italian cookbook authors, and her *Washington Post* article about her mother's cannoli served as the springboard for my cake. In the write-up, Domenica shared an easy yet stellar recipe for candied orange, which she has generously allowed me to reprint here.

MAKES ABOUT 2 CUPS

• Use a sharp paring knife to slice off the top and bottom of each orange. Score the oranges, making vertical slices at 1-inch intervals and cutting just through the peel and pith but not into the flesh. Pull off the segments of peel and slice them vertically into strips about ¼ inch wide. (Reserve the flesh for another use.)

• Place the peel strips in a medium saucepan and pour in enough water to cover them by at least 1 inch. Bring to a boil over medium-high heat, then reduce the heat to low and gently cook the peels for about 45 minutes, or until just tender. Drain in a colander.

• Set a wire rack on a rimmed baking sheet.

• Combine 1½ cups (300 g) of the sugar and 2 cups (475 ml) water in the same saucepan over medium-high heat; bring to a boil, stirring to dissolve the sugar, then reduce the heat to low and add the drained peels. Gently cook, stirring occasionally, for 45 to 60 minutes, or until the peels are tender and most (but not all) of the syrup has been absorbed. Use a slotted spoon to transfer the peels to the rack, taking care to keep them from touching. Let them dry for 1 to 2 hours. (Domenica recommends storing the remaining syrup in a jar in the refrigerator and using it to sweeten brewed tea.)

• Spoon the remaining ½ cup (100 g) sugar into a quart-size ziplock bag. Add 3 or 4 peel strips to the bag and shake to coat evenly. Place the coated strips back on the wire rack, taking care to keep them separate. Repeat until all the strips are coated. Let them dry overnight, turning them once or twice, before using or storing in an airtight container in the refrigerator for up to 1 month.

MARBLED MATCHA POUND CAKE WITH BERRY COMPOTE

1 cup plus 2½ tablespoons (225 g) granulated sugar

¾ cup (170 g) unsalted butter, at room temperature

6 ounces (170 g) cream cheese, at room temperature

1½ teaspoons finely grated lemon zest

1½ teaspoons vanilla extract

1½ teaspoons baking powder

1 teaspoon kosher salt

3 eggs, at room temperature

1¾ cups (225 g) all-purpose flour, plus more for dusting (see Note)

1½ to 2 tablespoons matcha powder (see page 139)

Berry Compote (recipe follows), for serving

Matcha, a finely milled green tea powder, adds a gorgeous swirl and lightly toasted, earthy note to this otherwise straightforward pound cake. Cut a slice and eat it plain, or serve it with berry compote—its brightness complements matcha's rich flavor—and maybe even whipped cream or ice cream.

MAKES 4 TO 6 SERVINGS

◆ Preheat the oven to 325 degrees F. Grease and flour an 8½-by-4½-inch or 9-by-5-inch loaf pan.

◆ In the bowl of a stand mixer fitted with the paddle attachment, beat the sugar, butter, cream cheese, zest, vanilla, baking powder, and salt on medium speed until light and fluffy, 4 to 5 minutes, scraping down the bottom and sides of the bowl often. Add the eggs one at a time, beating to fully incorporate after each addition and scraping down the bowl as needed. Reduce the speed to low and add the flour in two additions, beating until just combined. Scrape half of the batter into a medium bowl.

◆ Sift the matcha into the remaining batter in the mixer bowl. Mix on low speed until evenly distributed, no more than 10 seconds. Scrape down the bottom and sides of the bowl and use a silicone spatula to fold the batter once or twice if necessary to finish incorporating the matcha.

◆ Alternate spooning large dollops of each batter into the prepared pan. Rap the pan on the counter to even out the top. Insert a skewer or chopstick all the way down to the bottom of the pan and make six to eight figure-eight patterns throughout the batter.

NOTE: For an even lighter, more delicate crumb, substitute the all-purpose flour with 2 cups plus 3 tablespoons (275 g) cake flour.

◆ Bake the cake until a tester inserted into the center comes out clean, 70 to 80 minutes for an 8½-by-4½-inch pan or 60 to 70 minutes for a 9-by-5-inch pan. Allow the cake to cool for 30 minutes in the pan before running a knife around the edges of the pan and inverting the cake onto a wire rack. Cool completely before cutting slices and topping with berry compote.

Berry Compote

¾ pound (340 g) fresh or frozen berries, such as hulled and halved strawberries, blackberries, or raspberries

3 to 4 tablespoons granulated sugar

1 tablespoon plus 1 teaspoon water, divided

1 to 2 teaspoons freshly squeezed orange or lemon juice

Pinch of kosher salt

1 teaspoon cornstarch

¼ teaspoon vanilla extract

This versatile compote can also be made with chopped rhubarb or stone fruit.

MAKES ABOUT 1 CUP

◆ In a small saucepan, stir together the berries, 3 tablespoons of the sugar, 1 tablespoon of the water, citrus juice, and salt and bring to a simmer over medium-high heat. Reduce the heat to medium and simmer, stirring occasionally, until the berries have softened and released their juices, 8 to 10 minutes. In the final minute of cooking, in a small bowl, stir together the cornstarch and remaining 1 teaspoon water. Add the slurry to the pan and stir the mixture, while simmering, until thickened. Remove the pan from the heat and add the vanilla. Taste and add more sugar if desired. Allow the compote to cool, or serve warm spooned over cake. Store in an airtight container and refrigerate for up to 5 days.

BAKING WITH MATCHA POWDER

When baking with matcha, look for the less expensive culinary-grade variety (save the ceremonial stuff for drinking). It has a slightly different flavor profile but serves the same purpose for half the cost. It's available online and in most Asian supermarkets. For this cake, decide which amount of matcha to use based on how pronounced you want the flavor to be.

LEMON-LAVENDER YOGURT CAKE

1¼ cups (250 g) granulated
  sugar
3 tablespoons dried lavender
  buds
Finely grated zest of
  1 large lemon (about
  2 tablespoons)
1½ cups plus 2 tablespoons
  (210 g) all-purpose flour,
  plus more for dusting
2 teaspoons baking powder
1 teaspoon kosher salt
3 eggs, at room temperature
¾ cup (175 ml) neutral oil,
  such as canola or safflower
Scant ⅔ cup (155 g) full-fat
  plain or Greek yogurt, at
  room temperature
1½ teaspoons vanilla extract

For the lemon syrup
1½ teaspoons dried lavender
  buds
⅓ cup (65 g) granulated sugar
Freshly squeezed juice
  from 1 large lemon (3 to 4
  tablespoons)

This classic French yogurt gâteau is so simple, it's the first dessert many French children learn how to bake. Its toothsome, tender crumb is delicious on its own, but perfuming it with lavender (which reminds me of mesmerizing purple fields in the south of France) and bright lemon makes the cake truly transportive. The ingredients are traditionally measured out with a yogurt cup and mixed together in a bowl, but I've done the work of converting the recipe into more precise measurements. The zingy lemon syrup turns into a delightful crunchy coating as the cake cools. It might be my favorite part!

MAKES 4 TO 6 SERVINGS

• Preheat the oven to 350 degrees F. Grease and flour an 8½-by-4½-inch or 9-by-5-inch loaf pan.

• In a food processor, process the sugar, lavender, and lemon zest for 15 to 20 seconds, or until the lavender and zest are finely ground and have infused the sugar with their aroma and flavor. Alternatively, finely crush the lavender in a mortar and pestle and use your fingers to rub it and the zest into the sugar.

• Transfer the sugar mixture to a large bowl. Whisk in the flour, baking powder, and salt. Add the eggs, oil, yogurt, and vanilla and whisk until fully incorporated and a smooth batter forms. $\longrightarrow$

NOTE: If you don't like or can't find lavender, omit it. Skip the food processor and simply rub the zest into the sugar before proceeding as instructed.

◆ Scrape the batter into the prepared pan and bake until the cake is a deep golden brown and a tester inserted into the center comes out clean, 65 to 75 minutes for an 8½-by-4½-inch pan or 50 to 60 minutes for a 9-by-5-inch pan.

◆ Meanwhile, make the lemon syrup. Crush the lavender buds in a mortar and pestle and transfer them to a small bowl with the sugar. (Alternatively, process them in a food processor like for the cake, then transfer to a small bowl.) Add the lemon juice and mix to combine—the syrup should have a thin, runny consistency. Stir to combine again before using.

◆ When the cake is done baking, remove it from the oven and immediately spoon the syrup over the top. Allow the cake to cool in the pan for 30 minutes before running a knife around the edges of the cake and inverting it onto a wire rack. Cool completely before serving. The cake keeps well wrapped at room temperature for 3 to 4 days.

CHOCOLATE SOUR CREAM CAKE

1 cup (130 g) all-purpose flour
⅓ cup plus 1 tablespoon (40 g) natural cocoa powder, preferably high-fat (see Note)
½ cup (120 g) sour cream, at room temperature
¼ cup (60 ml) water
10 tablespoons (140 g) unsalted butter, at room temperature
½ cup (100 g) granulated sugar
½ cup (100 g) packed light brown sugar
1 teaspoon vanilla extract
1 teaspoon kosher salt
¾ teaspoon baking soda
½ teaspoon instant espresso powder (optional)
2 eggs, at room temperature
Powdered sugar, for dusting (optional)

For the glaze
5 tablespoons (70 g) unsalted butter
¼ cup plus 1 tablespoon (30 g) natural cocoa powder
½ cup (60 g) powdered sugar, sifted
½ teaspoon vanilla extract
1½ tablespoons very hot water

We all need an everyday chocolate cake in our lives. No buttercream, layers, or other frills—just a simple cut-and-come-back cake that's not too sweet, but perfectly moist and chocolatey. Baking it up in a loaf pan keeps it casual, and the straightforward ingredient list does too. I've added a rich, glossy glaze for when you're feeling a little extra, but the cake is quite perfect on its own with a simple dusting of powdered sugar.

MAKES 4 TO 6 SERVINGS

◆ Preheat the oven to 350 degrees F. Grease an 8½-by-4½-inch or 9-by-5-inch loaf pan and line the bottom with parchment paper.

◆ In a medium bowl, sift the flour and cocoa powder and whisk together to evenly distribute. In a small bowl, whisk together the sour cream and water.

◆ In the bowl of a stand mixer fitted with the paddle attachment, combine the butter, both sugars, vanilla, salt, baking soda, and espresso powder. Beat on medium speed until light and fluffy, 4 to 5 minutes, scraping down the bottom and sides of the bowl often. Add the eggs one at a time, beating to fully incorporate after each addition and scraping down the bowl as needed.

◆ Reduce the speed to low and add the flour mixture in three additions, alternating with two additions of the sour cream mixture, mixing until just combined and scraping down the bowl as needed. $\longrightarrow$

◆ Scrape the batter into the prepared pan and smooth out the top. Bake the cake until a tester inserted into the center comes out clean, 50 to 60 minutes for an 8½-by-4½-inch pan or 40 to 50 minutes for a 9-by-5-inch pan. Allow the cake to cool in the pan for 30 minutes before running a knife around the edges and inverting it onto a wire rack. Cool completely before dusting with powdered sugar or topping with glaze.

◆ To make the glaze, in a small saucepan, melt the butter over medium-low heat. Add the cocoa powder and stir to fully incorporate—the mixture should be smooth and glossy. Remove the pan from the heat and add, but don't stir in, the powdered sugar and vanilla. Gradually add the hot water, stirring to combine after each addition—it won't seem like the glaze is coming together at first, but eventually it will turn thick and glossy. Pour the glaze over the cooled cake (you won't use all of it) and allow it to set for 15 minutes before serving. The cake keeps well wrapped at room temperature for 3 to 4 days. Any leftover glaze can be stored in an airtight container and refrigerated for up to 1 week.

VARIATION: You can substitute half of the all-purpose flour with ½ cup plus 1 tablespoon (65 g) rye flour for an especially tangy, malty version. Alternatively, double down on the chocolate by folding ¾ cup (130 g) semisweet or bittersweet chocolate chips or chunks into the batter just before baking.

EARL GREY TEA CAKE

1⅓ cups (175 g) all-purpose flour, plus more for dusting

1½ teaspoons baking powder

¾ teaspoon kosher salt

½ cup (120 ml) cold heavy cream

3 eggs, at room temperature

1 cup plus 2½ tablespoons (225 g) granulated sugar, plus more for sprinkling

4 teaspoons (3 to 5 bags) Earl Grey tea leaves

1½ teaspoons finely grated lemon or orange zest

1½ teaspoons vanilla extract

¼ cup (60 ml) neutral oil, such as canola or safflower

On first glance, this dessert might pass for a lemon poppy seed cake, but upon further inspection, you'll quickly find that those dark flecks are actually Earl Grey tea leaves. They infuse the batter with bergamot oil and mingle with the vanilla and citrus zest—it's the sort of snacking cake that begs for an actual cup of hot tea to go along with it. If you're wondering what whipped cream is doing here, it's working magic, leaving the spongelike crumb light, airy, and soft. Greek yogurt, sweetened with a bit of honey and vanilla, makes a great accompaniment.

MAKES 4 TO 6 SERVINGS

◆ Preheat the oven to 350 degrees F. Grease and flour an 8½-by-4½-inch loaf pan.

◆ In a medium bowl, whisk together the flour, baking powder, and salt.

◆ In the bowl of a stand mixer fitted with the whisk attachment, whip the heavy cream until medium-firm peaks form. Scrape the whipped cream into another bowl and refrigerate while mixing the batter.

◆ Wipe down the mixer bowl with a paper towel, then beat the eggs and sugar on high speed until thick ribbons form (see page 42), 5 to 6 minutes. Add the tea leaves, zest, and vanilla and mix until just combined. Reduce the speed to low and gradually pour in the oil, mixing until just incorporated and scraping down the bottom and sides of the bowl as needed.

‣ Using a silicone spatula, fold the flour mixture into the batter in three additions until just combined. Fold in one-third of the chilled whipped cream to lighten the batter, then fold in the remaining whipped cream until just combined.

‣ Gently scrape the batter into the prepared pan and sprinkle the top with sugar. Bake until the cake is golden brown and a tester inserted from the side toward the center comes out clean (the top bakes up firm, making it hard to test from that point), 40 to 50 minutes. Allow the cake to cool for 30 minutes in the pan before running a knife around the edges of the pan and inverting it onto a wire rack. Cool completely before serving. The cake keeps well wrapped at room temperature for 2 to 3 days.

HONEYED FIG AND ANISE SEMOLINA CAKE

²/₃ cup (225 g) honey
½ cup (120 ml) freshly
squeezed orange juice
(from about 1½ medium
oranges)
½ cup (120 ml) water
10 to 14 fresh figs (about 10
ounces, depending on size),
destemmed and halved
1 cup (155 g) semolina flour
1 cup (130 g) all-purpose flour
2 teaspoons baking powder
1 teaspoon kosher salt
Finely grated zest of 1 medium
orange
2 teaspoons anise seeds,
crushed
1 cup (200 g) granulated sugar
2 eggs, at room temperature
2 egg yolks, at room
temperature
¾ cup (180 g) plain yogurt, at
room temperature
¾ cup plus 2 tablespoons
(200 g) unsalted butter,
melted and cooled
Thick Greek yogurt, for
serving

I wanted this cake to both capture the vibrant yet sultry essence of the Mediterranean as well as nod to the syrup-soaked semolina cakes found in that part of the world. What makes this dessert special is the orange-honey syrup that's used to poach the juicy, ripe figs and also sweeten and flavor the anise-flecked batter. Once out of the oven, the cake is soaked with the remaining syrup and eventually flipped to reveal the figs, sparkling like jewels.

MAKES 6 TO 8 SERVINGS

+ Preheat the oven to 350 degrees F. Grease a 9-by-5-inch loaf pan and line the bottom with parchment paper.

+ In a small saucepan, whisk together the honey, orange juice, and water. Bring to a boil and add the figs. Reduce to a gentle simmer, cover, and cook for 5 to 7 minutes, or until the figs are soft and tender. Use a slotted spoon to transfer the figs into a small bowl. Continue simmering the liquid until it thickens and coats the back of a spoon, about 15 minutes (it will continue to thicken as it cools). Measure out ⅓ cup (80 ml) of the syrup in a liquid measuring cup and chill in the freezer while you make the batter. Set aside the remaining syrup.

+ Arrange a single even layer of poached figs in the bottom of the prepared pan (if you have any extra, save them for a snack) and top with 3 tablespoons of the syrup. Set aside.

• In a medium bowl, whisk together both flours, baking powder, and salt. In a large bowl, use your fingers to rub the orange zest and anise into the sugar until it takes on their perfume and color. Whisk in the eggs, egg yolks, yogurt, and chilled ⅓ cup syrup. Gently whisk the flour mixture into the wet ingredients until just combined. Add the butter and whisk to incorporate.

• Carefully pour the batter over the figs in the pan (try not to disturb them) and smooth out the top. Bake until the top of the cake is set and the edges begin to brown, 35 to 40 minutes. Loosely cover the pan with aluminum foil and continue baking until the cake is golden brown and a tester inserted into the center comes out clean, another 20 to 30 minutes.

• Use a wooden skewer or chopstick to poke deep holes into the cake. Slowly and evenly pour the remaining syrup over the top. Allow the cake to cool for 1 hour in the pan before running a knife around the edges of the pan and inverting it onto a wire rack. Cool completely before serving it with a dollop of Greek yogurt. This cake is best the day it is baked, but it will keep well wrapped at room temperature for 3 to 4 days.

BAKING WITH SEMOLINA FLOUR

If you've ever made pasta from scratch, then you're familiar with semolina—a high-protein flour made from durum wheat. I love the way it adds rich, buttery flavor; a golden-yellow hue; and a fine, somewhat sandy texture to baked goods.

PARSNIP AND CRANBERRY MAPLE CAKE

2 cups (260 g) all-purpose flour
¾ cup plus 2 tablespoons (170 g) maple sugar
¾ cup (150 g) granulated sugar
1 tablespoon ground ginger
1½ teaspoons ground cloves
Rounded 1 teaspoon ground cinnamon
Rounded 1 teaspoon lightly packed freshly grated nutmeg
Rounded 1 teaspoon kosher salt
¾ teaspoon baking powder
¾ teaspoon baking soda
3 eggs, at room temperature
1 cup (235 ml) neutral oil, such as canola or safflower
⅓ cup plus 1 tablespoon (85 ml) buttermilk or plain yogurt, at room temperature
2 teaspoons vanilla extract
12 ounces (335 g) grated peeled parsnips (about 3 cups lightly packed)
1½ cups (155 g) fresh or frozen cranberries, roughly chopped
Unsalted butter, for griddling
Crème fraîche, for serving
Flaky sea salt, for serving

Move over, carrot cake, it's time for parsnip to step into the limelight. The "white carrot" holds an edge over its brighter counterpart in that its sweetness is nutty and spiced, making it a lovely wintertime alternative. For this one-bowl loaf, parsnips cozy up with a warm medley of spices and maple sugar, while fresh cranberries offer a pop of color and tartness. After a day or two, I like giving it the Whale Wins treatment: the Seattle restaurant griddles thick slices of their zucchini bread in butter and then serves it with crème fraîche and flaky sea salt—it's a game changer.

MAKES 6 TO 8 SERVINGS

• Preheat the oven to 350 degrees F. Grease a 9-by-5-inch loaf pan and line with parchment paper, leaving overhang on the long sides.

• In a large bowl, whisk together the flour, both sugars, ginger, cloves, cinnamon, nutmeg, salt, baking powder, and baking soda. Add the eggs, oil, buttermilk, and vanilla and whisk until fully combined and the batter is smooth. Fold in the parsnips and cranberries until just combined.

• Scrape the batter into the prepared pan and bake until the cake is a deep golden brown and a tester inserted into the center comes out clean, 75 to 90 minutes. Allow the cake to cool in the pan for 30 minutes before using the overhang to lift it out of the pan and transfer it to a wire rack. Cool completely before serving. The cake will keep well wrapped at room temperature for 4 to 5 days.

NOTE: To speed things up, use a food processor to both shred the parsnips and chop the cranberries. You can also serve this cake topped with browned-butter or regular cream cheese frosting (see page 88)—use a quarter portion of the recipe.

◆ To griddle the cake, cut a thick slice and generously spread butter on both sides. Cook it in a cast-iron skillet over medium-low heat until the bottom is golden brown, 3 to 5 minutes. Flip and cook the other side. Serve hot with a generous dollop of crème fraîche and a sprinkle of flaky sea salt.

ROASTED PUMPKIN SPICE CAKE WITH TAHINI GLAZE

1½ cups plus 1 tablespoon
   (200 g) all-purpose flour
2 teaspoons ground cinnamon
1½ teaspoons ground ginger
1 teaspoon kosher salt
1 teaspoon baking soda
½ teaspoon baking powder
½ teaspoon ground cloves
½ teaspoon ground cardamom
½ teaspoon lightly packed
   freshly grated nutmeg
2 eggs, at room temperature
½ cup plus 1 tablespoon
   (115 g) firmly packed light
   brown sugar
½ cup (100 g) granulated sugar
1½ teaspoons vanilla extract
¾ cup (175 ml) refined
   coconut oil, melted, or
   other neutral oil, such as
   canola or safflower
1 cup (240 g) canned or
   homemade pumpkin or
   squash puree, at room
   temperature
Pepita pumpkin seeds, for
   garnish
Black and white sesame seeds,
   for garnish

For the glaze

½ cup (60 g) powdered sugar,
   sifted
1½ to 3 tablespoons heavy
   cream or milk
4 teaspoons tahini
1 tablespoon maple syrup
   or honey
Pinch of kosher salt

This cake is what the British would call *moreish*. So positively delicious and pleasant to eat, you simply want more of it. The crumb is velvety and laced with just enough spice to bring out the subtle sweetness of pumpkin. It's finished with a nutty, slightly bittersweet tahini glaze and a sprinkle of sesame seeds and pepitas for crunch and a touch of glam. If you have the time and desire, roast and puree your own squash (see page 156).

MAKES 4 TO 6 SERVINGS

◆ Preheat the oven to 350 degrees F. Grease and lightly flour an 8½-by-4½-inch or 9-by-5-inch loaf pan.

◆ In a small bowl, whisk together the flour, cinnamon, ginger, salt, baking soda, baking powder, cloves, cardamom, and nutmeg.

◆ In the bowl of a stand mixer fitted with the whisk attachment, beat the eggs, both sugars, and vanilla on medium speed until thickened and pale in color, 3 to 4 minutes. With the mixer running, slowly pour in the oil in a steady, thin stream. Pause to scrape down the bowl, then gradually add the pumpkin puree one large spoonful at a time. Stop the mixer, scrape down the bowl, and then add the flour mixture all at once. Mix on low speed, scraping down the bowl as needed, until just incorporated. Use a silicone spatula to fold the batter a few more times to fully incorporate the flour. $\longrightarrow$

* Scrape the batter into the prepared pan and smooth out the top. Rap the pan against the counter a few times to remove any air bubbles. Bake the cake until a tester inserted into the center comes out clean, 60 to 70 minutes for an 8½-by-4½-inch pan or 50 to 60 minutes for a 9-by-5-inch pan. Allow the cake to cool for 30 minutes in the pan before running a knife around the edges and inverting it onto a wire rack. Cool completely before glazing.

* To make the glaze, in a small bowl, mix together the powdered sugar, 1½ tablespoons heavy cream, tahini, maple syrup, and salt to combine. The glaze should be thick but pourable. If it's too thick to pour, stir in more heavy cream 1 teaspoon at a time.

* Pour the glaze evenly over the cooled cake and garnish with pepitas and sesame seeds. Allow the glaze to set for 10 to 15 minutes before serving. The cake will keep well wrapped at room temperature for 3 to 4 days.

HOMEMADE PUMPKIN OR SQUASH PUREE

Winter Luxury pumpkin, kabocha, red kuri, and butternut squashes are some of my favorite varietals to bake with, adding a depth of flavor you can't find in canned puree. To make puree at home, preheat the oven to 375 degrees F and line a baking sheet with parchment paper. Cut the gourd in half and remove the seeds and pulp. Place the halves cut side down on the prepared pan and roast for 45 to 60 minutes, or until a fork or knife inserted into the thickest part easily pierces the skin and flesh. Allow them to cool completely before scooping the flesh into a food processor (discard the skins). Puree until smooth. The puree will keep in an airtight container in the refrigerator for 5 to 7 days or in the freezer for 2 to 3 months.

STICKY DATE AND GINGER CAKE WITH COCONUT-RUM SAUCE

1 teaspoon baking soda

8 ounces (225 g) pitted dates (a generous 1½ cups), preferably Medjool (see Note)

1 cup (235 ml) boiling water

2 to 3 teaspoons finely grated peeled fresh ginger (see Note)

1 teaspoon vanilla extract

1½ cups (195 g) all-purpose flour

1½ teaspoons baking powder

1 teaspoon kosher salt

5 tablespoons (70 g) unsalted butter, at room temperature

¾ cup (155 g) firmly packed dark brown sugar

2 eggs, at room temperature

Vanilla ice cream, for serving

For the coconut-rum sauce

6 tablespoons (85 g) unsalted butter

⅔ cup (135 g) packed dark brown sugar

¼ teaspoon kosher salt

⅓ cup (80 ml) full-fat coconut milk

2½ tablespoons light or dark rum

This English sticky toffee pudding is baked in a loaf pan instead of individual ramekins. It's rich and dense thanks to pureed dates and plenty of brown sugar, and even richer with the toffee sauce poured over. A bit of fresh ginger adds a subtle warmth to the cake, and coconut and rum (beware, it's got kick!) in the sauce play off of the tropical note. A scoop of vanilla ice cream is optional but highly encouraged.

MAKES 6 TO 8 SERVINGS

◆ Preheat the oven to 350 degrees F. Grease an 8½-by-4½-inch cake pan and line the bottom with parchment paper.

◆ In a deep small bowl, sprinkle the baking soda over the dates; pour the boiling water over them to submerge. Let the dates soften for at least 30 minutes. Puree the soaked dates along with their liquid, ginger, and vanilla in a food processor.

◆ Meanwhile, in a small bowl, whisk together the flour, baking powder, and salt.

◆ In the bowl of a stand mixer fitted with the paddle attachment, beat the butter and sugar on medium speed, scraping down the bowl and beater often, until pale in color and relatively fluffy, 4 to 5 minutes. Add the eggs one a time, beating to fully incorporate after each addition and scraping down the bowl as needed. Add the date puree and mix on the lowest speed until just combined. ⟶

NOTE: Medjool dates, with their deep, rich notes of butterscotch and maple syrup and soft texture, are my preferred variety for this cake. Also, I like the ginger to be subtle, but if you want yours to venture into gingerbread territory, use the full 3 teaspoons.

The batter will look curdled. Scrape down the bowl and beater and add the flour mixture. Mix until just combined. Use a silicone spatula to fold the batter a few times to make sure it's smooth and no lumps or residue remain.

◆ Scrape the batter into the prepared pan and smooth out the top. Bake for 55 to 65 minutes, or until the cake is dark brown and a tester inserted into the center comes out clean—a few crumbs are OK.

◆ While the cake is baking, make the sauce. Combine the butter, sugar, and salt in a small heavy-bottomed saucepan. Cook over medium heat, stirring often, until the butter melts and the sugar dissolves. Continue stirring until the mixture comes together and starts to simmer at the edges. Once the first bubble in the center comes up, set a timer and cook, stirring constantly, for 2 minutes (it will be very bubbly and puffy at this point!). Reduce the heat, carefully pour in the coconut milk, and bring to a simmer once more. Remove from the heat and allow to cool for a few minutes before stirring in the rum. Keep the sauce warm until ready to use—it will continue to thicken as it sits.

◆ Allow the cake to cool for 15 to 20 minutes before running a knife around the edges of the pan and transferring it to a serving platter. Pour half of the warm sauce over the cake. Serve the cake warm by the slice with the remaining sauce and a scoop of ice cream.

◆ The cake keeps well wrapped at room temperature for up to 5 days. The sauce can be made up to 1 week in advance and refrigerated; simply warm in a saucepan before using.

BRANDIED PERSIMMON TEA CAKE

1½ cups plus 2 tablespoons (210 g) all-purpose flour
1 cup (200 g) granulated sugar
1¼ teaspoons baking soda
¾ teaspoon kosher salt
¾ teaspoon ground cinnamon
½ teaspoon allspice
2 eggs, at room temperature
1 cup (255 g) persimmon puree, preferably Hachiya variety (see page 161)
⅓ cup (80 ml) neutral oil, such as canola or safflower
¼ cup (55 g) unsalted butter, melted and cooled
4 tablespoons brandy, cognac, or bourbon, divided
1½ teaspoons vanilla extract
1 large firm but ripe Fuyu persimmon
¼ cup (80 g) apple jelly or other light-colored preserve

I often find that with persimmon desserts, the fruit's sweet, delicate flavor (reminiscent of squash—in a good way!) is masked by too many spices and sweetener. To give the fruit its due reverence, persimmon is used in this recipe to both flavor the batter and to embellish the top. This autumnal cake also plays to the fruit's affinity for warmer flavors, like brandy, cinnamon, and allspice. Once baked, the persimmon slices are brushed with apple jelly, giving the humble cake a touch of glam.

MAKES 4 TO 6 SERVINGS

• Preheat the oven to 350 degrees F. Grease an 8½-by-4½-inch or 9-by-5-inch loaf pan and line it with parchment paper, leaving overhang on the long sides.

• In a large bowl, whisk together the flour, sugar, baking soda, salt, cinnamon, and allspice. Add the eggs, persimmon puree, oil, butter, 3 tablespoons of the brandy, and vanilla. Whisk to combine until a smooth batter forms. Scrape it into the prepared pan.

• Cut the persimmon into 5 slices and then halve the slices lengthwise for 10 half-moons. Arrange them, slightly overlapping, over the batter in one centered row. Bake until the cake is deep brown and a tester inserted underneath the fruit in the center comes out clean, 75 to 85 minutes for an 8½-by-4½-inch pan or 65 to 75 minutes for a 9-by-5-inch pan. Transfer to a wire rack.

◆ While the cake cools, in a small saucepan over low heat or in the microwave, warm the apple jelly until it liquifies. Let it cool a bit before stirring in the remaining 1 tablespoon brandy. Generously brush the jelly over the top of the cake and persimmon slices. Set aside the jelly.

◆ Allow the cake to cool for 30 minutes before using the overhang to lift it out of the pan and transfer it to a wire rack. Brush the sides with the remaining apple jelly. Cool completely before serving. The cake will keep well wrapped at room temperature for 4 to 5 days.

NOTE: The edges of this cake are prone to overbaking in a dark-colored loaf pan. Consider getting a light-colored pan (see page 8), omitting the persimmon topping, or baking at 325 degrees F—the baking time will be a bit longer. If you omit the persimmon topping, you can also serve this cake topped with browned-butter or regular cream cheese frosting (see page 88)—use a quarter portion of the recipe.

BAKING WITH PERSIMMONS

Persimmons are in season from October through January. Acorn-shaped Hachiyas ripen faster and get more jellylike than squat Fuyus; either works in the batter but make sure they're really soft. To make the puree, cut a deep slit into the bottom of each persimmon, scoop out the pulp, and then puree in a food processor until smooth before using in the batter.

ACKNOWLEDGMENTS

My first thank-you goes to myself for my prescient purchase of twenty-five-pound bags of flour and sugar just before the COVID-19 pandemic hit and grocery stores across the country emptied themselves of baking ingredients.

In all seriousness, though, writing this book was one of the hardest projects I've ever taken on, and to do it while a pandemic and civil unrest waged outside made it all the more challenging. Which is why I'm profoundly grateful for my community of friends and family, who listened to me almost exclusively brainstorm, analyze, extol, complain about, rejoice in, and stress over cake for an entire year. I couldn't have done it without your support.

I'd like to thank the following individuals:

My husband, Lee, who ate more cake in the past year than any human should have to. Without your discerning palate and insatiable sweet tooth, which conveniently overlapped with your seldom-wavering willingness to taste-test, these cakes wouldn't be as good as they are. I love you to the moon and back.

My Book Larder crew! Lara, who met my ever-changing schedule with understanding and flexibility. Amanda, who from the beginning saw my potential and helped it flourish. Jen and Mira, who tested for me and cheered me on, along with Dee Dee, Abby, Meghna, Megan, and the rest of the Book Larder community. I'm so blessed to have all of you in my life.

My editor, Susan Roxborough, who continues to be an absolute joy to work with. Thank you for giving me the shot—and then later on the push—I needed and for always being so gracious and amenable. I appreciate you. Also, a big thanks to Bridget Sweet, Anna Goldstein, Rachelle Longé McGhee, and the rest of the Sasquatch team for all their hard work in bringing this book to life. Charity, this book wouldn't be nearly as special without your exquisite eye and talent—you're the best.

My stellar recipe testers: Ana, Anna, Anthea, Colleen, Daniel, Daria, Ella, Emma, Izzy, Jacqueline, Jen, Katy F., Katy I., Kelsey, Libby, Lindsay, Linnea, Madison, Mira, Molly, Olga, and Talia. Thank you for putting up with my follow-up emails and messages and working through all the kinks with me—you guys rocked it. And, of course, a special shout out to Vanessa, who was always willing to be my sounding board and who should get as much credit for the tres leches cake as I do. I'm so grateful for that fateful Fat Llen brunch.

My mom and aunts, who taught me how to bake and who passed down their extremely discerning palates when it comes to dessert (their motto: "The more cream, the better!").

Lastly, thank you to all the countless people who I panned cake off onto. Whether you actually ate it or threw it away, ignorance is bliss.

INDEX

TO MY HUSBAND,
LEE, I LOVE YOU

"Candied Orange Peel" by Domenica Marchetti/Domenica Cooks LLC. Used by permission.

Printed in China

SASQUATCH BOOKS with colophon is a registered trademark of Penguin Random House LLC

26 25 24 23 22   9 8 7 6 5 4 3 2 1

Editor: Susan Roxborough | Production editor: Bridget Sweet
Designer: Anna Goldstein | Photographer: Charity Burggraaf
Food styling: Polina Chesnakova

Library of Congress Cataloging-in-Publication Data
Names: Chesnakova, Polina, author.
Title: Everyday cake : 45 simple recipes for layer, bundt, loaf, and sheet
   cakes / Polina Chesnakova.
Description: Seattle : Sasquatch Books, [2022] | Includes index.
Identifiers: LCCN 2021024217 | ISBN 9781632172983 (paperback) | ISBN
   9781632172990 (ebook)
Subjects: LCSH: Cake. | LCGFT: Cookbooks.
Classification: LCC TX771 .C458 2022 | DDC 641.86/53--dc23
LC record available at https://lccn.loc.gov/2021024217

ISBN: 978-1-63217-298-3

Sasquatch Books | 1325 Fourth Avenue, Suite 1025 | Seattle, WA 98101

SasquatchBooks.com

FSC
www.fsc.org

MIX
Paper from
responsible sources
FSC® C001701